This book is dedicated to my friend Michael Kile,
with love and appreciation for his faith in me.
I'll miss you, Michael.

Doll on facing page by Virginia Robertson

CLOTH DOLLS

How to Make Them   Miriam Gourley
The Quilt Digest Press

Editorial and production direction by Harold Nadel.
Book and cover design by Kajun Graphics, San Francisco.
Photography by Sharon Risedorph, San Francisco.
Typographical composition by DC Typography, San Francisco.
Printed by Nissha Printing Company, Ltd., Kyoto, Japan.
Color separations by the printer.
Line drawings by Mary Ellen Brown.

First printing.

Library of Congress Cataloging-in-Publication Data

Gourley, Miriam, 1951-
    Cloth dolls : how to make them / Miriam Gourley.
        p.   cm.
    Includes bibliographical references.
    ISBN 0-913327-32-8 (ppr) : $19.95
    1. Dollmaking 2. Soft toy making 3. Doll clothes   I. Title.
TT175.G68   1991
745.592'21—dc20   91-26644
                                                        CIP

The Quilt Digest Press
P.O. Box 1331
Gualala, California 95445

ACKNOWLEDGMENTS

There are several people who have given invaluable help during my book-writing experience. I would like to thank Judy Duncan for knowing WordPerfect so I didn't have to take a crash course. I'm grateful to Mary Ellen Brown for her willingness, her enthusiasm and her beautiful drawings. I want to express my admiration and gratitude to Harold Nadel for his editorial brilliance and the privilege of working with him. Finally, I thank my dear husband, Bruce, and our children for their patience and support while I was hovering over my computer.

TABLE OF CONTENTS

INTRODUCTION

This book includes the work of ten main dollmakers plus cameo appearances by several other dollmakers who have contributed their distinctive techniques in creating dolls from the Basic Rag Doll pattern in this book. No two dollmakers approach dollmaking alike. Some may begin with sketches, some with the development of the pattern shapes, and others are inspired by the fabric. Some dollmakers may spend a longer time in the "birth" phase than the "gestation," and others may develop new ideas based on previous designs. Whatever the actual approach, the final ideas are here for you to enjoy, to create from and to learn from.

The instructions are included to enable you to make replicas of the pictured dolls; however, I encourage you to bring the elements of your own personality into this process. Choose your favorite colors, fabrics, laces, trims, embellishments, hair colors and fibers. Do not be afraid to vary from the pattern by painting a face which the designer has embroidered, or vice versa. Some grade-school teachers may have admonished us to "stay within the lines." I encourage dollmakers to depart from the instructions and try new ideas. I hope this kind of creative freedom will eventually inspire dollmakers to create dolls without the use of patterns.

Designing a cloth doll is the process of combining many elements, including texture, color and fabric, to achieve a particular effect. Designing with fabric is very exciting to me: fabric is such a large part of our everyday life. We drape our windows with it, we cover furniture with it and we wear it every day. Fabric is a very natural medium for art. Somehow, dollmaking is also an extension of mothering for me. Just as all of my children have distinct personalities, so do the fabric people I create.

My childhood on a farm provided fertile places for my imagination to grow. In the spring and summer, as we brought the cows home to be milked in the evening, we passed by a beautiful stream where the willows grew by the bank. In the midst of the stream, two or three little islands had formed. We pretended that fairies and elves lived there. I suppose all of these experiences help explain why much of my work centers around Oriental art, fairies, fantasy figures and storybook characters.

In my early years, most of Santa's gifts to me were dolls. Each one was cherished and played with until most of its hair was gone and its clothes were faded and tattered. Dolls have always been a pleasurable part of my life. My sister Sonia shared this love for dolls. As we grew, Barbie and her friends became a very important part of our play. We sewed countless ball gowns and bedding, decorated plywood

houses with our homemade furniture, and saved all our money to buy accessories. We spent many hours inventing wonderful adventures for these dolls.

During my teenage years, doll playing was replaced by boys and other interests. When I was in my mid-twenties, at home with my own little boy, I bought a sewing machine and re-discovered the pleasure of sewing. With my background in art, I felt a great urge to experiment and create designs of my own. At that point, I bought a commercial doll pattern. I wanted to diverge from the cover model, so rather than use the cute face drawn by the pattern designer, I drew my own. I used very large plastic eyes, painted an arty nose and mouth, and sewed clothing from my scrapbox.

I took the doll to a beautiful gift shop which specialized in hand-made items, hoping to make a grand entrance into the world of designing. The owner looked at the doll and told me my craftsmanship was a little weak. She also pointed out the incongruity between the dramatic face and the cute, little-girl-style clothing. The focus on craftsmanship made such an impression on me that I began paying much more attention to details such as stuffing the doll so it wasn't lumpy, making sure seams didn't pucker, and working with facial details until they were right for the doll. I began to look for new techniques to strengthen my skills.

With this dubious beginning, you might wonder why I continued making dolls. As a child, I checked out as many doll books as I could find. Two, in particular, stood out in my mind. The first was a story about a tiny doll, about the size of a thumb, who accidently fell from the toy shelf and was devoured by the vacuum cleaner. Through a series of accidents, she ended up in a jar of jelly. The little girl who owned the doll became sick. To cheer her up, the child's mother went to the pantry to find some jelly for the child's toast. When the mother discovered the little doll peering out at her from inside the rosy jelly, she unmolded the jelly, doll and all, and served it to the little girl in her sickbed. I always had a fantasy about owning tiny dolls like the one in the story. When I first saw Lucy, pictured on page 97, I was especially charmed by her. She's just the size to be captured in jelly.

The second story was Rumer Godden's *Miss Happiness and Miss Flower*, about two Japanese dolls. They belonged to two little English girls—Belinda, a naughty, spoiled child, and her orphan cousin, Nona, who had recently come from India. The story told how, through the efforts of making a Japanese doll house, the cousins eventually became good friends. After reading the story many times, I struggled to make a Japanese house like the one in the book. I managed to construct part of it, but I did not have the materials, money or skills to complete it.

Part of the appeal of these two stories was the fact that both were told from the dolls' point of view. That only helped reinforce my opinion that dolls have feelings, too.

As I began to develop my dollmaking skills, I began to study about other dollmakers. I discovered there were few famous cloth-doll makers throughout history. However, as I became acquainted with many of the current artists, particularly the ones whose work has a primitive or folk-art look, one American dollmaker's name was mentioned several times. That dollmaker was Izannah Walker. She was one of the first to produce cloth dolls; she patented them in 1873, but she had possibly been producing them since the 1840's. Her dolls are very much in demand by collectors, who consider them the most desirable American cloth dolls.

The great French clothing designer Erté also designed dolls. This Russian-born Paris-based artist, who was christened Romain de Tirtoff, is best known for his fashion and theater designs. From 1919 to 1936, Erté furnished the readers of *Harper's Bazar* with illustrations of the latest creations from Europe. His clothing designs were characterized by their seamless construction, but his unique accessories, such as doll-shaped handbags, a screen with marionettes above it and boudoir dolls, were also part of his creative distinction. He once said, "I have always felt that dolls, if they are beautiful, should be displayed as works of art."[1]

Cloth dolls have become a way of expressing feelings and viewpoints. Doll artist elinor peace bailey (who prefers no capital letters in her name), from Hayward, California, discusses this aspect of the creative process: "Finally, I had found my language. The dolls brought me the love that I hungered for. The audience I began to acquire through them permitted me to be myself. The dolls, who could not be burdened with my anger nor, at this point, with any heavy messages, did not threaten people. I was listened to through the dolls."[2] elinor has become a modern cloth-doll advocate. She flies all over the country to lecture and teach workshops. She also was partially responsible for starting a very successful cloth doll club in her town.

My approach to dollmaking is broken down into two main processes. The first is the longer, and it begins with an idea. The idea may come from an illustration, a trip to the local doll museum where a particular doll may be the springboard for a new idea, a conversation with a fellow designer, or a beautiful piece of fabric. As this seed begins to take form in my mind, I start the mental assembly of the doll. One of the important elements in this process is the construction. For instance, in designing a new doll pattern for a client, I was inspired by some Americana-style fabric. I designed an Uncle Sam whose proportions were like Uncle

---

[1] Stephanie Farago, *The Magic and Romance of Art Dolls* (Los Angeles: Farago Publications, 1986), p. x.

[2] Elinor Peace Bailey, *Mother Plays With Dolls* (McLean, Virginia: EPM Publications, Inc., 1990), pp. 10-11.

Sam on stilts. As I began to think of the stilts, I wondered about putting wood inside the legs to give the appearance of the lanky legs and to give a different weight and feel from a doll filled with stuffing. Thus, a line of dolls called "Skinny Bones" began, starting with Uncle Sam and Betsy Ross, followed by Pecos Bill, Calamity Jane and a long, lean Victorian doll.

Many times after I'm in bed, which is one of the few quiet times of my day, I work out construction techniques in my mind. I have a good idea of how the doll will be constructed before I cut into the fabric. I also try to visualize how the finished doll will look—or at least the important elements of his/her personality. I rarely make very detailed drawings, because the finished doll usually doesn't resemble the drawing.

To many people, much of the joy of creating a doll is collecting the various accessories and embellishments that make a doll unique, that give it a personality of its own. This is another very important part of this first process, which I call the "gestation" of the doll. I begin to look for materials to construct and enhance the personality of the doll, such as fabrics, trims and embellishments. When I knew, for instance, that I wanted to create a romantic Victorian doll for this book, I wanted her to be rather unconventional, like me—maybe even a little eccentric. I didn't want to use colors that a more sedate doll might wear. I called this style "funky Victorian" and began to collect turquoise tulle spangled with silver, sea-green moiré-printed cotton, gold-edged wired peach ribbon to make roses, rich paisleys with black background, deep navy blue with wine-red roses, metallic threads to quilt the jacket, sea-green and lavender beads for accents, all of which would show off the wonderful carrot-top mohair doll hair. I laid them out in two combinations, hoping to select the one I liked better for this book. I liked them both so well that I decided to make two sister dolls.

When the fabrics and trims were all assembled and their construction was complete in my mind, they were ready for the second phase—"birth." This phase was begun by drawing pattern pieces, drawing and re-drawing faces, and cutting the muslin for the bodies. There are many steps between the birth and the ultimate presentation to the public. Somewhere in between quilting their coats and working on their hats, I knew Bernadette and Marguerite were hatmakers. It seemed only natural, as the two of them seemed to enjoy watching me create their hats!

This birth process is a combination of all the technical aspects of creating a doll. This consists not only of working on the pattern, painting or drawing a face, sewing the body, stuffing it, selecting hair fiber and color (even creating your own color, for the truly adventurous dollmaker), and attaching the hair to the doll's head. Another part of this process is selecting and creating clothing for the doll. That is a very enjoyable process for me, particularly the embellishment of clothing. Fabric manipulation is a very satisfying though painstaking part of dollmaking. New fabric can be created by quilting, pleating, embroidery (as on the Princess Bride, page 65), beadwork, dyeing and painting.

This book is designed as a text for dollmakers. I have included information for all skill ranges. If you have never made a doll before, you can easily make the Basic Rag Doll in Chapter 1. In fact, you should make several, to practice various techniques of creating a face, applying different kinds of hair and dressing the doll utilizing several embellishment processes. Intermediate dollmakers will enjoy making Anne of Green Gables, Mary Ruth or Becky Tuttle's Victorian doll. The Princess Bride will challenge the advanced dollmaker.

Whatever your skill level, if you are a serious dollmaker, look through the list of tools and supplies and accumulate as many as possible. Organize an area for your work space. Purchase cardboard drawers for your glue guns, paints, ribbons, buttons, floss, needles, thread, beads and other tools. Put up open shelves to store your fabric right where you can see it and be inspired by it. Clear off your work table, plug in your sewing machine, and get ready to play!

Chapter 1
BASIC DOLLMAKING INSTRUCTIONS

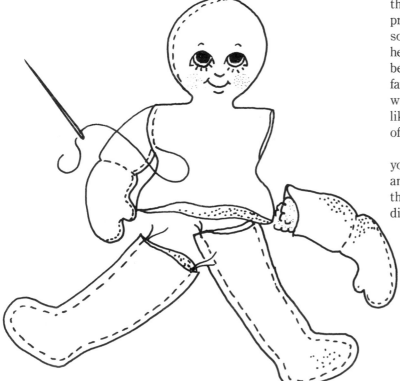

his chapter will introduce you to dollmaking tools and supplies and the Basic Rag Doll pattern. This pattern creates a very simple gingerbread-man doll, a dress and pantaloons. The pantaloon pattern may also be used for pants, if you prefer to create a male doll. Several doll artists of varying skills were invited to use this pattern, interpreting it in their own way. These artists include professional designers; since I wanted to showcase all skill levels, several children were also invited to make dolls. I know you will enjoy looking at all the interpretations.

I believe it is important to include a simple, uncomplicated rag doll in this book. Simple dolls are charming and can become a child's most beloved belongings. If you are attempting to create your first doll, it is best to start with a simple pattern. This Basic Rag Doll is simple enough that a child may be taught to sew it, and it is the right size. However, if you are making it for a very young child, embroider or paint the features rather than using buttons, which may be chewed off and swallowed. If you paint the fabric, choose a non-toxic paint. Pre-wash the fabric to remove all sizing and chemicals before you begin work on the doll.

This Basic Rag Doll will be able to cross gender barriers. This pattern can be used in grade school by boys and girls as an art project. Men and women, boys and girls can all try their hand at creating. This would also be an enjoyable project for senior citizens or those who are handicapped in some way. Cub Scouts could make their favorite superheroes, young girls in 4-H might enjoy making a ballerina before watching *The Nutcracker* at Christmas time, or your family might enjoy doing self-portraits, just for fun. You may wish to make one of these dolls to decorate for each holiday, like Susan Hale's Miss Liberty, page 32, to celebrate the 4th of July.

This chapter includes basic instructions to assemble your doll body—cutting out the fabric, stitching, stuffing and assembling. Doll hair instructions are also included—the kinds of fibers available, making wigs, or applying hair directly to the head.

The art of dollmaking has improved over the last few years, due in large part to the availability of new tools, computerized sewing machines, varieties of thread colors and textures, incredible fabrics, acrylic paints in all kinds of colors and textures, and new materials such as Sculpey®, a clay which can be hardened in your oven. You will see Sculpey® used as a mask on Susanna Oroyan's Basic Rag Doll, page 25. Permanent-ink fine-tip marking pens are also available in a myriad of colors. Early dollmakers were restricted not only by cost but often by limited selection and availability of supplies.

I encourage you to study the various techniques described in this chapter. If you have previously embroidered all your doll faces, try painting them for a change. If you have used wool roving only in the packaged colors, try dyeing your own shade. Experiment with fibers you haven't tried before. Dollmaking should be enjoyable: more than that, it should be a time for creative freedom. Remember, you don't have to "color within the lines"!

TOOLS AND SUPPLIES

Basic Sewing Kit
Embroidery, quilting, blunt craft and 3 1/2" dollmaker's needles
Needle threaders
Pincushion with straight quilting pins
Safety pins (small)
#2 Lead pencils
Colored pencils
Iron-on transfer pencil
Sulky® Iron-On Transfer pen
Permanent-ink fine-tip marking pens
Crayons
Tracing paper
Paper scissors, pinking shears, fabric shears, small embroidery scissors
Rotary cutter
Rotary mat
Crochet thread
Sewing thread (cotton/polyester blend, quilting)
Decorative thread for machine (rayon, metallic)
Embroidery floss
Embroidery hoop

Tweezers
Bamboo skewers, 3 1/2" hemostat, bamboo chopsticks (extra long)
Various sizes of dowels for stuffing
Glue gun, glue sticks, white tacky glue
Paper-backed fusible webbing
Measuring tape

Painting Supplies
Acrylic paints, textile medium (to dilute paints)
Sta-set Fixative
Brushes of various sizes, from #00 up to 3/4" wide
Acrylic clear matte sealer (spray and brush-on)
Round wooden toothpicks
Container for water (to clean brushes after changing color)
Sponge brush
Paper towels (to dry brushes after dipping in water)
Mixing tray or palette
Blow dryer to shorten drying time

Doll Body Materials and Supplies
Unbleached muslin or other suitable flesh-colored fabric
Rit® Dye to tint fabric and hair fiber, if desired: cocoa, golden yellow, tan, rose pink and tangerine
Cotton batting
Polyester filling
Black tea bags (to tint fabric)
Colander (to drain fiber)
Screen (for drying fiber)
Cotton swabs
Pink or peach powder blush

Fiber for Doll Hair
Curly wool crepe
Wool roving
Nubby yarn
3-ply natural hemp rope
Naturally curled, dyed mohair
Various yarns
Natural flax
Camel hair

Miscellaneous Supplies
Buttonhole twist
Jute, twine

TINTING FABRIC FOR DOLL BODY

TINTING MUSLIN PINK

A1 There are many fabric colors available for doll bodies. Many dollmakers use unbleached muslin, but others prefer a little more pink color. You may find the pink color you wish to use; if not, here's a recipe for tinting muslin:

One-half yard or less of muslin may be tinted pink, using this recipe.

1/8 teaspoon Rit® Dye (Rose Pink)
1/4 teaspoon Rit® Dye (Tangerine)
3–4 quarts hot tap water

Mix the dye and water together until the dye is dissolved. Place the fabric in the dye bath. Stir every few minutes, checking the color until the desired shade is reached. Squeeze out excess water and rinse the fabric in cool water. Place the fabric in the dryer to heat-set the color, and press it.

TEA-DYEING FABRIC

A2 Tea-dyeing is a very common and easy way to tint fabric to look old. Fabric may be tea-dyed before cutting out the pattern or after the body is sewn (prior to stuffing). Tea-dyeing may also be used on clothing fabric. One and one-half yards or less of muslin may be dyed using the following recipe:

Pour two quarts of very hot tap water into a large bowl, add 15 tea bags and steep 20 minutes. Remove the tea bags. Place the fabric in a bowl and soak 30 minutes, stirring the fabric occasionally if you wish the color to be even. Squeeze out excess tea. Place the fabric in the dryer to help set the dye. Press the fabric. Rit® Dye (Tan) may also be used for the same effect as tea-dyeing.

PATTERN LAYOUT

Method 1
TRACING THE BODY DIRECTLY ONTO FABRIC

B1 1. Some pattern instructions indicate pattern pieces should be traced onto the wrong sides of the fabric. Fold the fabric, selvages together, and trace around pattern pieces with a #2 pencil, or use tracing paper to trace pattern pieces onto fabric without having to cut pattern pieces out. You will only trace

outer perimeters of fabric pieces, not the facial details.

2. Place the fabric on your sewing machine and stitch on the penciled lines, leaving the openings as indicated. Do not stitch the face or the head pieces until you ascertain whether the face will be embroidered, painted, etc. Set the stitched pieces aside. (See E3 for stitch length guides, trimming seam allowances and clipping curves.) Transfer all the markings and facial details as listed below at B4-B6.

Method 2
CUTTING OUT THE DOLL BODY

B2 1. Fold the fabric so the right sides are together, selvages together. Pin the pattern pieces to the fabric. If you plan to embroider the doll's face, cut all other pieces out and set them aside. Trace around the head or head/torso (for one-piece construction) on the right side of the fabric. Transfer all the markings.

B3 2. Before removing pattern pieces from the fabric, make tailor tacks if necessary. For example, tailor tacks should be made to indicate stitch lines or construction guides, such as circles on patterns or dart lines. Tailor tacks are made as follows:

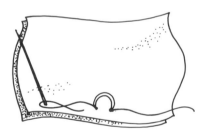

TRANSFER METHODS

B4 **Simple Tracing** Place the fabric on a light table or against a window and trace directly from the pattern, with a #2 lead pencil. This method is the best if you don't have any of the following supplies. It is the most difficult with which to achieve accuracy.

B5 **Tracing Paper** Use tracing paper by placing the paper, coated side down, on the right side of the fabric. Place a pattern piece on top of the tracing paper and use a pencil to trace the facial features. Press firmly, but don't poke holes through the paper. This method is easy and reliable, but you need to be sure your tracing paper is as close as possible to the embroidery floss color you will use, or as neutral as possible so it won't show through your embroidery.

B6   **Transfer Pens and Pencils** The Sulky® Iron-On Transfer pen is a black-ink permanent pen that is used to trace the doll's features onto tracing paper or other semi-transparent paper. After the ink dries, the paper is placed, ink side down, onto the fabric. Use a hot iron (at cotton setting or less, if the fabric tends to scorch). Press for 20-30 seconds, lift the iron and check to see if the markings are dark enough. The only problem with this pen is the difficulty in drawing thin lines. If you need thinner lines, release some ink onto a piece of paper by pressing the tip of the pen for a second. A puddle of ink will appear, and you can use a round toothpick to draw details onto the paper. I personally think this pen is perfect for painted faces, such as Marguerite's and Bernadette's, page 107. The pen gives enough graphic detail that paints may be used to fill in the color. Transfer pencils work in much the same way as the pen, but you are able to get finer details. When ironed, however, the markings spread slightly. Embroidery covers the marks satisfactorily.

CREATING THE DOLL'S FACE

PAINTING

There are two main types of paint, oil base and latex (water base). Both types are used in dollmaking; however, latex or acrylic paints are most often used. They have several distinct advantages over oil, especially minimal drying time and clean-up with soap and water.

Acrylic Paints

C1   There are many good brands of acrylic fabric paints on the market. It doesn't matter what kind you buy, since the basic chemical makeup is about the same. There are many different varieties, textures and colors, however. I have found that paints which are specified for fabrics are better for dollmaking, but artists' acrylic paints may be thinned to the right consistency with a little experimentation. Following is a list of some of the paints available in quilt, fabric and craft stores which may be used in dollmaking:

Fabric Paints Acrylic paints specifically mixed and used on fabric. These come in a variety of colors and hues. Some are plain, some are shiny and wet-looking when dry, and some dry to a matte finish. (Clear acrylic varnishes may be used to achieve a shiny finish, if they are applied after the fabric paints are dry.)

Metallic Although these paints may have a metallic sheen, they have no metal content. They may be thinned with water, but I recommend a textile medium (see below). Metallic paints look especially dramatic on darker fabrics.

Textile Medium A water-based, colorless medium used to thin acrylic paints. It helps prevent bleeding beyond painted lines: if water is added to thin acrylic paints, sometimes the color will crawl across the fabric. Medium also helps you to blend and move colors more easily on fabric. Colors can be lightened or thinned in intensity by adding medium. There is no exact ratio of medium to acrylic paint. Some artists dip the brush in the medium and directly into the dye. Some like to paint part of the design in medium on the fabric and, while it's still wet, apply the acrylic paint.

Fixative A clear solution that helps acrylic paint retain its intense color even when thinned to water consistency. It prevents a lightly painted area from fading through repeated washing. Fixative may be used to create watercolor effects (see C4).

Glitter Paints A milky acrylic paint base mixed with colored glitter. When the paint is dry, the paint base is clear. Glitter paints may be mixed with other colors, or thinned for sparkly eye shadow, lip color or cheek color. Sally Lampi's ballerina version of the Basic Rag Doll (page 21) shows good use of this product.

Glue Paints Recommended for children who are painting dolls or art projects. When dry the paint is permanent, but if the child accidently spills glue paint on clothing, it can be washed out, if done so immediately.

Oil Paints

C2   Helen Pringle is one of the few dollmakers who use oil paints to create doll faces. She approaches dollmaking from a very traditional perspective. As a collector of antique dolls and furniture, Helen particularly admires the dolls of Izannah Walker. Helen likes the soft, old look oils give a doll. She has developed a unique process to achieve this look, and she has used this technique on her Basic Rag Doll (page 32).

Helen's process uses something she calls "Miracle Messy Mixture," which prevents her carefully painted doll heads from permanently denting. This process is not for the beginner, but using the Basic Rag Doll pattern is an excellent way to explore this technique. The process is as follows:

1. Mix one part Liquitex® Acrylic Modelling Paste and one part Liquitex® Acrylic Gel Medium (Acrylic Matte Medium could be used in place of the Gel Medium, but the Gel Medium makes a smoother mix which doesn't show brush marks). Buy the smallest sizes you can get, as the paste begins to harden once it is opened. Use a good brush, preferably a 3/4″ soft nylon exploded-tip, as it seems to minimize brush marks and cleans easily. The mixture should be combined in a small glass jar with a tight-fitting lid and a mouth wide enough to admit the brush easily. A pimento jar is about right. Water may be added sparingly, a few drops at a time, when the mixture begins to thicken. If too much water is added, adhesion will be poor and the coating will eventually crack. Once the paste has been opened and partly used, wipe the top edge clean to avoid having dried bits fall into the jar and ruin the remaining paste. Before replacing the lid, cover the mouth of the paste jar with a square of plastic wrap to make a tighter seal. Mix only the amount that you will use within a few days, and seal the mixture jar with plastic under the lid, also.

You must work quickly, as the mixture begins to dry when it is exposed to air. If the brush becomes clogged, swish it in water and press the excess out with a paper towel. Clean the brush in water between coats. You should use a minimum of four coats, letting the first coat dry two hours and each subsequent coat one hour. Clean up with soap and water.

2. After the second and all subsequent coats, sand carefully with a small square of medium sandpaper or a coarse sponge-back flexible sanding pad to eliminate brushmarks and rough spots. Wear a dust mask and work outdoors if possible, as the fine dust will settle on everything. If the head is to have a wig, the part to be covered need not be sanded. Hair can also be built up and modeled on the head with the application of extra coats of the mixture to that area. When the head is coated to your satisfaction, paint it with either oils or acrylics.

Specific Painting Techniques

C3 You may wish to sew and stuff your doll head prior to painting; however, this is not law. Many dollmakers prefer to paint the faces before stuffing, as painting on a flat surface is easier for them. Painting before stuffing has one drawback: when you turn the face right-side-out after sewing, the paint may become crinkled.

Assemble all your paints and cover the table surface with newspapers or cardboard. You may also wish to protect your clothing by wearing an apron. Acrylic paint is difficult to remove from clothing, even

if it is freshly spilled. Collect the following supplies and place them on your work table:

Mixing tray or palette (to mix paint colors)
Paper towels, used to roll around wet brushes to remove excess water after changing colors
A wide selection of brushes
Paints, fixatives, textile medium, etc.
Hair dryer, to lessen drying time
Two or three small containers, such as small paper cups to mix color wash in.

C4 **Color Wash** Using a color wash (or watercoloring) can highlight areas of the doll's face—a light blue wash around the eyes, a light red wash for the cheeks, and a coffee stain to highlight contours of the face (paint strong coffee directly onto a doll's face which you previously wet with fixative). The cheek color on Bernadette and Marguerite (page 107) was applied with this method. Sally Lampi's ballerina (page 21), made from the Basic Rag Doll pattern, is also a good example of a color wash.

1. Pour fixative in a small bowl. Place acrylic paint on your palette. Dip a large brush into the fixative and wet the doll's face. This will prevent color from bleeding or wicking into other sections. Do not let the fixative dry. Add a small amount of the desired color

to the to the fixative in a small container. You will not use much paint to add color to the fixative. Apply the mixture to the doll's cheek or other area of the face with a soft brush. You may also add glitter paints to the wash, but you need to stir it often and dip your brush frequently while applying it to the doll's face. The more fixative you use, the less intense the color. When it is dry, the color tends to darken, so apply less color than you wish to see ultimately.

2. When the wash is dry, you can add detail and line work, again with paint and a fine liner brush. Permanent-ink fine-tip marking pens may be used first to draw the design.

C5   **Painting Facial Details**   All instructions for doll patterns in Chapter 3 include a diagram of the face. Included in the diagram are the paint colors specified in the Materials List for each doll. You will notice that different brands of fabric paints were used. *You may freely substitute other brands.*

Follow the paint diagrams carefully, and start at the top of the face unless otherwise directed. If you start at the lips, for example, and work toward the eyes, you may accidently brush your hand on the wet paint and smear your work.

Before you paint anything, I recommend that you mix the paint and try it on a scrap of the muslin used for the doll's face. For example, if you use tea-dyed muslin, the colors will look different than on unbleached muslin.

I recommend a small brush (#00 or #0) for painting eye details, such as the iris and pupils. For very fine detail work, such as the face of the Princess Bride (page 69), use the tip of a round toothpick or pin to trace the eyes, lashes and nose area.

As with any other skill, practice as much as you can. When I was first beginning to paint faces, I cut out several heads or head/torsos and painted them all. I chose the best to use on the doll.

OTHER METHODS OF COLORING DOLLS' FACES

Permanent-Ink Fine-Tip Marking Pens, Colored Pencils, and Crayons

C6   Dirk's facial features (page 123) were created by using a brown permanent-ink fine-tip marking pen to draw the details, then colored pencils were used to color the eyes and mouth. The doll's creator, Margaret Peters, used the seam to keep the face centered. After the eyes and mouth were colored, she added powdered blush, applied with a cotton swab, to color the cheeks.

Cindy Extance, who designed Felicity and Lucy (page 97), used a black permanent-ink fine-tip marking pen to outline the details, then she used violet, pink and red crayons to color in the eyes and mouth. A red permanent-ink fine-tip marking pen was used to outline the outer lip area. elinor peace bailey uses a blue permanent-ink fine-tip marking pen to outline her doll's eyes, and she also uses crayons to color the cheeks. The secret to using crayons for cheek color is to use a light hand. If you press too hard, your doll will end up with waxy cheeks.

Crayons and colored pencils are an excellent way to achieve a very soft look. Permanent-ink fine-tip marking pens are useful to give definition to facial features with reasonable accuracy.

When using any of the permanent-ink fine-tip marking pens, draw as quickly as possible without sacrificing accuracy. If you rest the pen too long in one area, the line will begin to spread or wick into the fabric. These pens are available in a variety of colors and may be purchased at quilting, craft, and fabric stores.

Embroidery

C7   Anne of Green Gables (page 139), by Christine Shively, is beautifully embroidered. Embroidery is a very traditional way of creating a doll's face. It may also be used in combination with other methods, such as permanent-ink fine-tip marking pens and powder blush. A good example of this is Becky Tuttle's Victo-

rian doll. She has embroidered the iris of the eye and the lips and used permanent-ink fine-tip marking pens to draw the details of the face.

As I said earlier, embroidery is more easily done before the face is stitched and stuffed. Using a hoop keeps the fabric taut, ensuring more even stitching. Following are general instructions for embroidery:

Fabrics Since dollmaking usually employs a fine weave rather than a coarse fabric, it is wise to line the fabric with a second layer. This will keep the knots and tails on the underside from showing through. These are most noticeable after the doll is stuffed. Lining the fabric will prevent this problem.

Needles Generally, it is best to use the smallest needle possible, to prevent large needle holes which can weaken the fabric. The needle size will also depend on the number of threads going through the eye of the needle. Most dollmaking can be done with sizes 5 to 8 embroidery needles.

Hoop Select a hoop large enough to encompass the entire design. Place the screw or clamp of the hoop in the 10 o'clock position (or 2 o'clock position, if you are left-handed) to keep the threads from catching.

Floss Cut the floss into 18″ lengths, run it over a damp sponge and separate all six strands of floss. Put back together the number of strands recommended in the instructions. If the floss becomes twisted, drop the needle and allow the floss to unwind itself. (Doll face diagrams will indicate the number of strands, for example 2 strands for satin stitching and 1 strand for outline.)

Back Stitching Complete all embroidery stitches before working back stitches or accent stitches. You will generally use one strand less than for the rest of the stitches.

Cutting the Floss Knot each section of face or embroidery work and cut the floss, rather than carrying floss from one eye to the next, for example. Dark threads are especially noticeable and will show through the fabric.

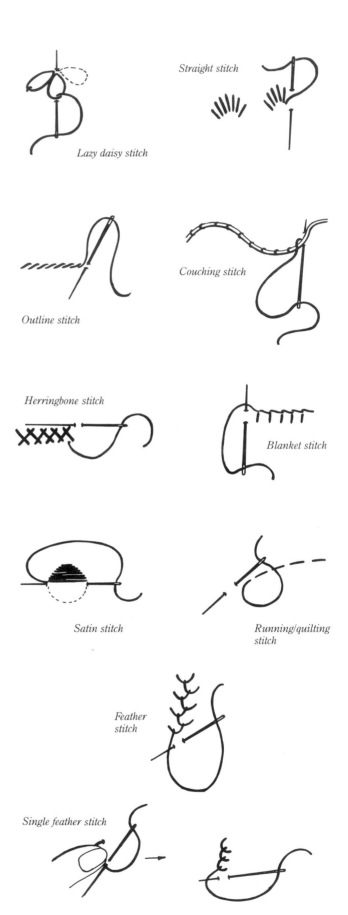

Straight stitch

Lazy daisy stitch

Outline stitch

Couching stitch

Herringbone stitch

Blanket stitch

Satin stitch

Running/quilting stitch

Feather stitch

Single feather stitch

C8

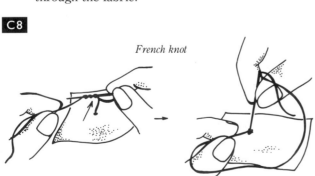

French knot

SCULPTURAL FEATURES

D1 elinor uses separately cut-out and sewn lips and nose for her doll's features (page 57). Her shortcut method also works beautifully for dimensional clothing decorating (such as hearts or fish shapes).

1. Cut the nose and mouth from appropriate fabrics. With right sides of nose pieces together, stitch completely around the nose WITHOUT leaving an opening through which to turn.

2. Cut a slit on one side of the nose, being careful not to cut through both layers of fabric. Trim the seam allowance to 1/8″ and turn the nose right side out. Stuff the nose through the slit you made. The slit will not have to be sewn shut, because it won't be seen. Follow the same procedure with the mouth, stuff it lightly and top-stitch across the center of the mouth.

3. Hand tack the nose and mouth in place. Overcast the nose a couple of stitches at the top and bottom of the nostrils to give them shape.

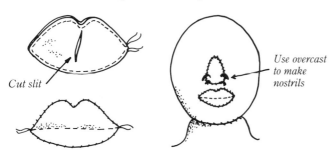

Cut slit

Use overcast to make nostrils

MISCELLANEOUS

D2 As you will see in the picture of Susanna Oroyan's version of the Basic Rag Doll (page 25), she has made a face for her doll using ceramic clay which is hardened in a regular oven, at a much lower temperature than a kiln. Using Sculpey® is no more difficult than baking cookies. She describes its uses and gives detailed instructions in her book (see "Additional Reading," page 159).

APPLIQUÉD CLOTHING

D3 If you are creating a doll with appliquéd underwear, you will need to apply this before you stitch your doll together. Machine appliqué is very simple, and elinor employs it frequently in her creative process.

1. Cut out the appliqué piece (for example, the front undergarment). Pin it onto the doll's front as indicated in the pattern piece.

2. Machine baste it in place, 1/8″ or less from the edge. This will give extra strength during stuffing.

3. Set your machine to the zig zag stitch (whatever width you wish). The length should be set at or near the buttonhole setting.

4. Stitch the appliqué (zig zag stitch) to the doll body, covering the basting. (This method may be used to appliqué socks, shoes, etc.)

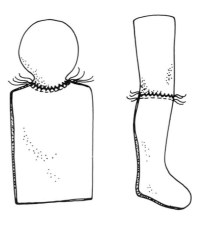

ASSEMBLY

Before you stitch the body together, some dolls need to be assembled. Bernadette and Marguerite (page 107), for example, have bodies stuffed as single pieces; however, the upper torso is made of muslin, from the waist to the top of the boots is a printed or solid fabric (to save making separate underwear), and the boots are muslin, later painted. The steps are as follows:

E1 1. Place the front torso and the lower body piece right sides together. Stitch across the waist. Press toward the lower body. Repeat for the back of the body. (See illustration on next page).

E2 2. Place the lower leg and the boot right sides together and stitch across the top seam allowance of the boot. Repeat for the back side. Press toward the lower body. Now you are ready for the next step.

STITCHING THE DOLL BODY TOGETHER

E3 1. Use 1/4″ seam allowances throughout, unless otherwise specified. Stitch the darts if the pattern has indicated them and place the pieces with the right sides together. Stitch around the body pieces, leaving openings as indicated. Stitch length should be about 16 stitches per inch. Smaller stitches help to increase the strength of seams when the doll is stuffed. For smaller hands, with individual fingers, such as those on the Princess Bride (page 65), you will want to make your stitch length the smallest possible and turn the wheel by hand, one stitch at a time, placing the needle exactly on the traced line.

2. Trim the seam allowance, especially on the face, to 1/8". Clip curves and angles as illustrated.

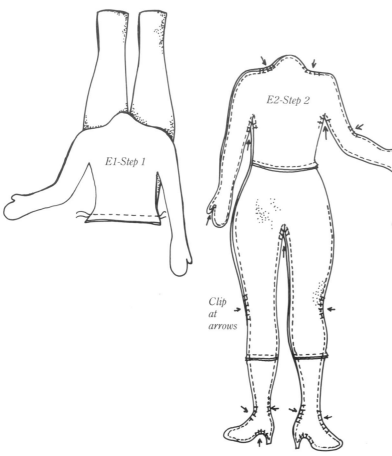

E1-Step 1

E2-Step 2

Clip at arrows

3. Turn the body part right side out with a long chopstick or dowel. For extra-small body parts, such as the hands on the Princess Bride (page 65), use tweezers to turn the hand right side out, then push the fingers out with bamboo skewers. Be very careful not to push too hard or you may rip through the ends. Push the chopsticks along all seams, especially small curved areas. There is no need to press the body, because stuffing will stretch the fabric and smooth any wrinkles.

STUFFING THE DOLL

E4   One of the most important techniques in dollmaking is the stuffing of the doll. No matter how beautifully the face is embroidered or how lovely the clothes are, the effect can be ruined by sloppy stuffing. Wrinkles along the chin or lumpy arms and legs will detract from the doll's appearance.

There are many brands of stuffing. You will need to try several and find the brand that works best for you. Most of the stuffing fibers are man-made, usually of polyester fibers. In many brands, the fibers are combed; thus the fibers run in one direction and are prone to matting and bunching. Fibers which take on a random arrangement after processing have extra resilience. These are easier to mold, they work into corners, and they give a smoother appearance to the finished project. The combed fibers are sometimes rolled into a batt; the random fibers usually expand when you open the package. Pull out a wad of stuffing; if it seems to string, and the fibers are all running in one direction, it may be the combed fiber. A handful of the random fibers will be more popcorn-shaped and will not have the fibers stringing from it.

GENERAL GUIDELINES

1. Assemble the tools you plan to use. Choose a tool that fits the cavity you are stuffing and can be held comfortably. You will probably want to include the following:

Dowels of varying widths, to use in larger areas to be stuffed

An extra long chopstick (for stuffing tubular pieces)

3 1/2" hemostat (from hospital supply source) used to grab small amounts of stuffing to place in hard-to-reach spots

bamboo skewers, to poke stuffing into small areas

a supply of stuffing

a flat work surface, such as a table.

2. Begin by fluffing small amounts of stuffing (stretch it in several directions) so it doesn't form a ball that may make a lump.

3. Push the stuffing firmly into the doll body, pushing into outer curves and angles until the stuffing is firm. (The exception to stuffing firmly is if the doll is for a small child and you may want it to be a bit more cuddly.)

4. Add small amounts of stuffing at a time. You never want to see where one piece of stuffing ends and another piece begins. This can be especially noticeable in legs and arms.

5. Gradually work from the outside edges toward the middle of large body pieces. Continue stuffing, using your free hand to flatten as you stuff. This helps prevent too much roundness.

*Clockwise from top: Virginia Robertson, Miriam Gourley,
Margot Strand-Jensen, Sally Lampi, Virginia Avery,
Sally Lampi, Vanessa Gourley*

E5   6. There are three methods of creating the appearance of fingers in a doll's hand. (A) Top-stitch the hand first, then stuff each finger and thumb afterward. (B) Insert a small amount of stuffing into the hand. If you insert too much stuffing, it may break your sewing-machine needle. Top-stitch the fingers using the pattern piece for a guide. (C) Stitch individual fingers, such as those of the Princess Bride (page 65).

E6   7. If the arm or leg you are stuffing is to be stitched into the torso, stuff the arm or leg to within an inch or less of the top edge. If you have difficulty stitching the arm or leg into the torso, remove a little of the stuffing and try again. If the arm or leg is not to be inserted in the torso, stuff it until it is firm and stitch the opening closed.

TROUBLESHOOTING GUIDE

E7

Problem	Solution
Wrinkles along the chin line	Add more stuffing, small amounts at a time, and push it toward the wrinkles with a chopstick or small dowel.
Body too round	As you are stuffing the body, flatten the stuffed piece with your free hand.
Lumpy appearance	Remove stuffing, re-fluff it and insert it slowly and carefully, using smaller amounts at a time.
Ripped seam	You are using too much force when pushing the stuffing into place.
Floppy body	You need to stuff more firmly. Add more stuffing, small amounts at a time.
Wrinkled neck (for one-piece head/ torso construction)	You may need to flatten the head and neck more while stuffing. The neck may not have enough stuffing.

NEEDLE SCULPTURE

In addition to top-stitching fingers (E5), which elinor does by inserting a small amount of stuffing, then top-stitching before stuffing the remaining fingers, she needle-sculpts to create a palm. This is accomplished by the following method:

E8   1. Using crochet string and a 3 1/2″ dollmaker's needle (with no knot), take the needle through the palm of the hand to the wrist. Make a small anchoring stitch at the wrist. Bring the needle back through the center of the stuffing to the palm, pulling slightly to form the palm. Go back and forth, from the wrist to the palm, about three times. Re-enter the wrist, then go out at the back of the wrist. Form a loop and pull the thread through it to make a knot. Pull it tight and re-enter the wrist to bury the thread. Clip it off.

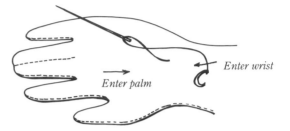

Enter palm   *Enter wrist*

E9   2. Elbows, shoulder, hip and knee joints are sometimes formed by partially stuffing the limb and machine stitching across the joint. elinor uses this method for her doll (page 57), and the Basic Rag Doll is jointed at the shoulder using this method.

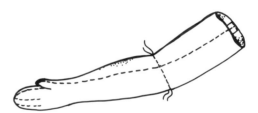

E10   3. To needle-sculpt a nose after the face is stuffed, lightly pencil the nose area onto the face. Insert a needle, then make a small anchor stitch at the top of the nose. Push the needle under the fabric and some of the batting, to the other side of nose. Push the needle back to the other side, pulling taut. Continue working in this manner until you reach the round area below the nose. Use a running stitch to gather the rounded area, then work back up the nose using the same procedure as before. Make a knot and hide the tail of thread inside the face.

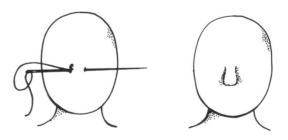

ATTACHING THE HEAD

Method 1
SEPARATE HEAD ATTACHED TO NECK TAB

E11 Some dollmakers hot-glue doll heads to the neck tab on the torso. I do not recommend this method, as it is difficult to keep the glue from showing. Also, if the doll is in a hot environment, the glue may melt and her head will fall off. If you wish to glue a doll's head, I recommend white tacky glue. Pin the head in place while it is drying.

Most dollmakers prefer to stitch the head to the body by hand. This seems to fasten the head more securely, without the risk of glue showing. It also allows for re-positioning, if the head is not attached correctly.

1. Use a strong thread, either sewing silk or quilting thread, with a narrow, long needle. Pin the head onto the torso. Adjust it as necessary, using the photo of the doll as a guide.

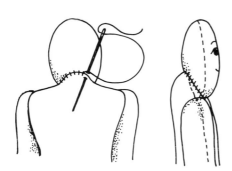

2. Begin at the back of the neck and whip stitch the head to the neck tab. Continue stitching around the head, under the chin and back around up to the neck tab. You may want to stitch around twice, for extra strength.

3. If the head is floppy, you need to stitch about 1/8″ away from the previous stitching, starting at the back of the neck and working around the doll's neck and chin area, as you previously did.

Method 2
NECK TAB INSERTED INTO THE HEAD

E12 1. Stuff the neck very, very firmly after stuffing the torso. The top of the neck needs to be rigid. Hand stitch the opening closed.

2. Cut a slit in the back of the head, noting the pattern for placement. (The head should be stuffed rather firmly.) With a dowel, push the stuffing aside and up; push the neck in, twisting it. Insert quilting pins through the head to secure it. Start stitching at one side of the opening and work around the neck.

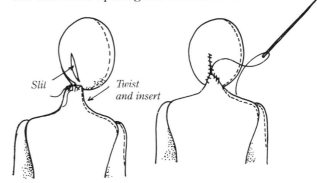

Slit   *Twist and insert*

Method 3
INSERTING THE HEAD/NECK INTO THE TORSO

E13 Method 3 is almost the exact reversal of Method 2. elinor peace bailey uses this method in her doll construction. After the head and torso are stitched, turned and stuffed, prepare the torso by moving the stuffing from the center where the neck will be inserted. Push the neck into the torso opening, making sure the raw edges of the torso are turned inside. Approximately two inches of the neck should be above the opening. Starting at the lower front edge of the neck, stitch all around the neck edge.

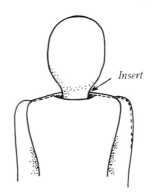

Insert

ARMS AND LEGS

Method 1
INSERTING ARMS AND LEGS INTO THE UNSTUFFED TORSO

E14 This is a simple construction method. The floppy limbs will keep the doll cuddly and old-fashioned. Insert the arm into the side opening of the unstuffed doll body. Top-stitch to hold it in place. Sew the top ends of the legs to the bottom of the body front, matching the raw edges. Take care to position the arms and legs correctly when sewing them to the body. Stuff the body firmly, using a dowel or chopstick. Take care to avoid splitting the seams. Hand stitch the body opening closed.

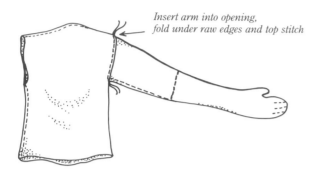

Insert arm into opening, fold under raw edges and top stitch

Method 2
INSERTING ARMS AND LEGS INTO THE STUFFED TORSO

E15 Stuff the torso first, turn under 1/4″ of the open end of the torso and insert the stuffed legs. Stitch across the bottom of the torso, making sure the legs are stitched into the seam. Insert the arms by folding in 1/4″ of the torso arm openings and top-stitch across these openings.

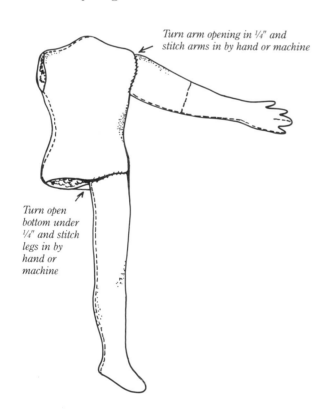

Turn arm opening in ¼″ and stitch arms in by hand or machine

Turn open bottom under ¼″ and stitch legs in by hand or machine

Method 3
ARMS AND LEGS ATTACHED WITH BUTTONS

E16 Using a button on the outside of an area will prevent threads from cutting through arm/leg fabric and causing the limb to fall off. This method also creates a slightly jointed effect.

1. After the limbs are stuffed and the opening has been stitched closed, place an arm on the doll with its thumb forward.

2. Place a 3/8″ button on the outside of the upper arm near the shoulder and tack it to the arm with quilting thread. Push the needle through the entire body (from shoulder to shoulder). Attach the other arm with a button, then go back and forth through the entire body about four times, trying to stitch through the same area each time. Pull the thread taut with each pass.

3. Repeat for the other limbs.

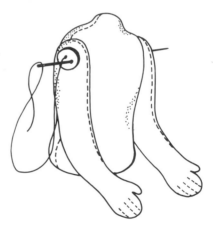

Method 4
ARMS AND LEGS STITCHED ONTO THE TORSO

E17 With this method, it is easier to achieve more sculptural detail. It is used for more advanced projects, such as The Princess Bride (page 65). There is no mobility of arm movement for this doll.

1. After the torso is stuffed firmly and the head attached, the arms are stuffed firmly, to within 1/2″ or less from the top. The raw edges are folded under 1/4″ and basted.

2. Pin the arms to the shoulder, adding a small amount of stuffing if needed. Use a bamboo skewer to insert small amounts of stuffing into the arms between the pins until the shoulders are firm and rounded. Hand stitch the arm to the shoulder.

3. Repeat this procedure for the legs, attaching them at the bottom of the stuffed body. Remove the basting.

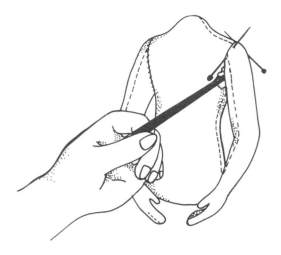

4. (Alternate method) After the arm is stuffed and all raw edges of the opening are stitched closed, attach the finished arm to the shoulder by taking a few stitches and leaving the arm dangling loosely (See Becky Tuttle's doll, page 149).

FIBERS FOR HAIR

FI Doll hair can be made from almost any fiber. There are a few synthetic fibers used; some are made into doll wigs which are frequently used in porcelain doll-making. Some synthetic fiber is curled and packaged loosely so the dollmaker can make her own doll wig. The synthetic fibers come in a variety of colors and they retain their original curl and color after a lot of handling. Yarns made from synthetic fibers such as acrylic and nylon may also be used in dollmaking. They are especially appropriate if the doll belongs to a child and will be washed frequently.

Most contemporary dollmakers do not use synthetic fibers for doll hair. Natural fibers are more congruent with the fabric generally used in cloth dollmaking. The doll's hair should enhance the overall feeling of the doll. Using a shiny nylon wig on a muslin doll is like using a yarn wig on a beautifully finished porcelain doll. If you create a doll from fabric, carefully working on each step of construction, the fibers and techniques of creating the doll's hair should have equal thought and time.

There are several natural fibers used in dollmaking, primarily the following:

Raw Washed Fleece Fleece is sheared from sheep or other animals, including goats, alpaca and camels. It may be washed to remove the undesirable characteristics of raw wool such as dirt and grease. There are many breeds of sheep and a variety of natural colors. Wool, however, is easily dyed to any

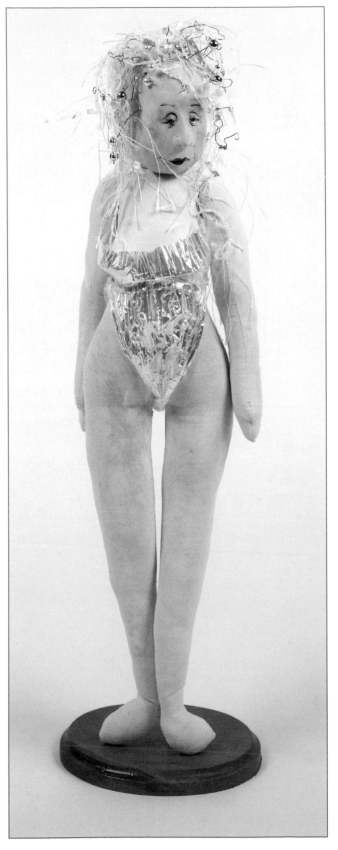

Susanna Oroyan

color. The length of the fleece fibers also varies for the different breeds of animals.

Roving Natural fleeces which have been washed are then carded by hand or machine to even the fiber lengths and form a batt. Roving, which is the name of the resulting product, is more homogenized than raw fleece and lacks the interesting curl and texture of some raw fleece. However, it is readily available and is used by many dollmakers with very good results.

Curly Crepe Wool Hair Wool fibers may be woven onto twine to achieve curly hair for dolls. This crepe fiber is often used in theatrical costume shops as well as for doll hair. It is simply unbraided and pulled apart slightly to fluff the fiber. It is then stitched or glued directly to the doll's head. It may also be re-braided.

Yarns After fiber is carded or otherwise processed, it is twisted into long strands. This process is called spinning, and the resulting product is yarn. Yarn is commonly used for weaving, knitting, crocheting, tapestry making, needlepoint and other needlework arts, but it also makes unique doll hair. Yarn can have a great variety of texture and color. Some may have a nubby texture, called bouclé; others are spun into varied widths with very narrow sections and very wide sections. Natural-fiber yarns are usually more expensive than man-made fibers, but all kinds make interesting doll hair. Cindy Extance (page 97), elinor peace bailey (page 57) and Christine Shively (page 139) all used yarn for doll hair with very good results.

Flax, Hemp and Silk Flax and hemp both come from plants. Flax is the raw product from which linen is made. I used natural flax to create the Basic Rag Doll on page 21. It can be easily dyed, but not easily curled. Its texture is much like real hair and it is fun to style.

Hemp is used to manufacture rope. When unwound and dyed, it may be used for doll hair. Roxanne Becker's beautiful Mary Ruth (page 87) has hair made from hemp rope. The texture is somewhat more wiry than flax.

Silk, from the domesticated silkworm, has a very soft texture, but it is a very strong fiber. Its tendency to become a little tangled makes it a bit more difficult to work with, but it can be easily dyed and the texture is wonderful to touch.

Torn Strips of Fabric Several designers used torn fabric strips to create hair for the Basic Rag Doll. Virginia Avery, Sally Lampi and Virginia Robertson (pages 21 and 3) used this method but managed to achieve a diversity of hair styles. If you wish to try this method, simply tear fabric into strips, as wide or narrow as you wish, and stitch them to the head as desired.

CURLING HAIR

F2 Wool, mohair, camel hair and other animal fibers may be curled. Dampen the fiber and wind it around a wooden dowel, pencil or cocktail pick, depending on the size of curl you desire. Do not wind too much fiber at a time: the greater the thickness, the less the curl. Let the fiber dry thoroughly overnight. Slide the curl off. You may clip off the length you need, and the curl may be glued or stitched in place.

Some synthetic fibers will curl a little. Test a small sample by wrapping the fiber around a dowel very tightly and immersing it in boiling water for about 30 seconds. Remove it from the water and let it dry completely.

DYEING DOLL HAIR

Man-made fibers will not absorb much, if any, color and will not generally produce satisfactory color changes. Natural fibers are the best candidates for customized color.

F3 If you want only a subtle color change, use tea or coffee. Lighter shades of wool, flax, mohair, etc. will stain nicely. Pale yellow, gray or natural-colored fiber will take on a rich brown hue. If you use silk, however, the color will be absorbed more quickly; in addition, silk is more heat-sensitive and must not be dyed as long.

Color small quantities at a time; about one yard of natural fiber is ideal. Bring a strong tea recipe to a boil (see A2), then reduce it to a simmer. Wet the fiber before adding it to the tea. Simmer for 10-30 minutes, depending on the color intensity desired.

Do not stir the fiber, as you may cause matting. Gently lift the fiber into a colander and let it drain naturally, without squeezing. This will give the fiber a chance to cool slowly. If you place boiling hot fiber into a cold pan of water without allowing it to cool first, it will lose its natural resilience. (Wool is especially prone to this problem.) Rinse the fiber in warm water and drain it again. When most of the water has been drained, spread the fiber on a screen or piece of stretched fabric, turning it from time to time so it will dry evenly.

F4 Commercial dyes also work well on animal and plant fibers. To dye hemp the color used on Mary

Ruth (page 87), use the following recipe:

Purchase 1 Box Rit® powdered dye in each of the following colors—Tangerine, Golden Yellow and Cocoa Brown. Dissolve the dye in one quart of very hot tap water. If using wool, wet it before you place it in the dye bath. Immerse the unravelled hemp rope in the mixture. You won't have to wait very long for it to acquire the proper color. Remove it and blot the excess water, using paper towels; hang it outside to dry. (Hemp doesn't curl well, but it may be braided, then dried, for a crimped look.) While you have the dye, you may want to experiment with other fibers. Try flax, mohair and silk, dyeing one at a time. Let the fiber dry thoroughly, at least overnight.

F5 You might also like to try using natural dyes for hair color. Many dollmakers like to experiment with this method of dyeing, letting it become part of the creative process. Natural dyes tend to fade, since they are not colorfast. In addition, the colors tend to deteriorate when exposed to light. When using natural dyes, you must use a mordant. A mordant is what makes the dye bond to the fiber. Commercial dyes, such as the dye used in the recipe above for Mary Ruth's hair, contain a mordant. Natural dyes do not contain a mordant, so you will need to include this step before the dye bath. This is called a pre-mordant.

Vegetable fibers, such as cotton and linen, need to be simmered and soaked in washing soda and a bit of detergent before dyeing. This allows the fibers to open and take dye better. Wool can be treated with the following pre-mordant: For one pound of wool, mix 3/4 oz. of alum and 1 oz. cream of tartar in 3/4 gallons of water. Bring it to a simmer, not a boil, in a porcelain-coated, stainless steel or copper pot. Add the wool and simmer it for 20-30 minutes. Treating silk in a pre-mordant is optional.

After you have finished the pre-mordant process, you may leave the fiber in the pre-mordant overnight and dye it the next day, or remove the fiber, drain it in a colander, and place it directly into the dye pot. Do not squeeze the fibers. Use a wooden spoon or dowel to lift it from one pot to the next. Drain as you would for the tea-stained fiber. Handle it as little as possible. Since you are immersing the fiber in boiling dye, the fiber must be wet before you place it in the dyepot.

If you would like to experiment with natural dyeing, use the following recipe, which produces a bright, clear yellow:

Onion dye
1 lb. onion skins
4 gallons of water

Soak the onion skins overnight, then simmer them 20 minutes. Remove the skins with a slotted spoon. Add wet, mordanted fiber and simmer it 10-15 minutes. Rinse, drain and dry it completely. Wash it in a mild detergent to keep the color from rubbing off the fiber.

If you are dyeing silk, simmer it only five minutes, then let it stand overnight. Rinse, then spread it out to dry.

There are many people who can assist you if you need further information about dyeing fiber. If you cannot find local experts in dyeing, see "Additional Reading" on page 159.

HAIR-MAKING TECHNIQUES

If you desire, you may pencil a hairline on your doll's head. You can then paint the hair color over the same area to prevent bald spots from showing through the hair fiber. After the paint is dry, make hair for the doll using one of the following methods.

Method 1
MAKING A SEPARATE MUSLIN-BASE WIG

F6 This method may be used for many hair fibers, and it takes less time than stitching hair to the doll's head by hand. This method is used for Bernadette's and Marguerite's hair (page 107).

1. Cut a muslin square to fit the doll's head. To decide what size square the doll will need, measure from the front hairline, up the center of the head and back down to the middle of the back of the head, as illustrated.

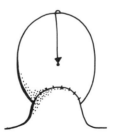 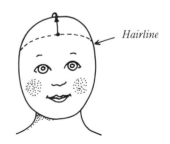

Hairline

2. You may use wool roving, acrylic fleece, silk, mohair, flax or nubby yarns.

3. Pull strands apart or cut the fiber into designated lengths. In the instance of the natural-curl mohair used on Bernadette and Marguerite, the fibers come in assorted lengths and do not have to be cut. Other fibers will need to be measured into lengths, using the following method to figure: measure from the top center of the doll's head (in the part-

line) to the length of the finished hairstyle; double the length. Using this number (Measurement A), cut three or more lengths. The number of lengths will depend on the ability of the fiber to cover the doll's head. If you use too little, you will have bald spots showing; if you use too much, the doll's hair will be too bouffant and may be hard to style. Other fibers such as natural-curl mohair may not be available in long lengths. When I made Bernadette and Marguerite, I used about l/2 oz. of the natural-curl mohair for each doll.

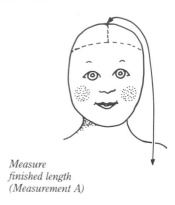

*Measure
finished length
(Measurement A)*

4. Place the muslin square beneath the center of the strands of fiber.

Mohair The longest strands of natural-curl mohair will be centered over the muslin; shorter pieces will be placed with the blunt (cut) ends slightly off center of the muslin, overlapping the center line. Continue adding the strands of mohair until 3/4 of the mohair is used. The remaining mohair will be used later.

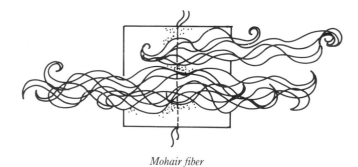

Mohair fiber

Curly Wool Crepe, Flax, Hemp, Yarn Depending on how many lengths of Measurement A you need to cover the doll's head adequately, place these lengths, one at a time, next to each other, centered over the square of muslin, as illustrated above.

5. Top-stitch by machine down the center of the square, with fibers running perpendicular to the line of stitching.

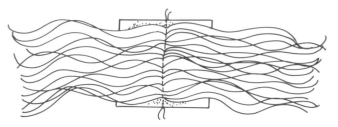

Flax, curly crepe wool, hemp or synthetic fiber

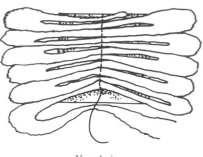

Yarn hair

6. Fold the square in half, with the stitching in the center of the fold and the muslin on the outside of the fold. Machine stitch next to the folded edge. This will hide the first stitching so it won't show when the square is opened up, and it will look more like a natural part.

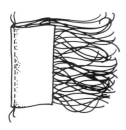

7. Clip all the threads. Trim the square to a football shape with the pointed ends at the ends of the stitching.

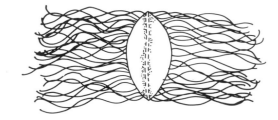

8. Pin the wig on the doll's head, noting the pattern for approximate placement. You may use a white tacky glue or hot glue to attach the wig to the doll's head. Glue one section at a time, lifting up the front wig section and gluing it first. Do not glue the back yet. If

you use a hot-glue gun, use a piece of cardboard to press the hair to the doll's head, to avoid burns.

9. You may either place glue on the back of the doll's head and press some of the fiber down to cover the bald spot (note illustration) or do step 10 below.

Glue front down

Hair glued in back

Glue

10. Measure across the bald spot at the back of the head (Measurement B). Cut a piece of muslin which is Measurement B by 3/4″. Press under 1/4″ of the width of Measurement B (the muslin will now be 1/2″ wide). With the folded edge away from you and the fold on the bottom, place the blunt fiber edges (if both ends of fiber are blunt, either end may be placed here) on the raw edge of the muslin. Machine stitch 1/4″ from the raw edge. Bring the folded edge of muslin over all raw edges and zig zag stitch. Trim off the loose threads. Glue the strip to the doll's head, about halfway up the back of the head. Glue the top section of hair to the head, covering the horizontal piece of muslin.

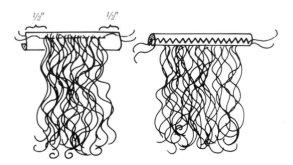

1/2″   *1/2″*

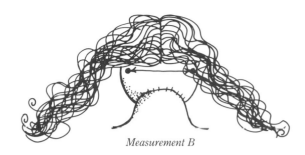

Measurement B

11. Rather than making a vertical strip of hair, you can tie a thread around a small hank of hair and glue it to the back of the head just below the point where the football-shaped end will be. Glue the back of the wig over the hank of hair.

12. Style as illustrated:

Style for the Princess Bride (Pull hair away from face, trim ends)

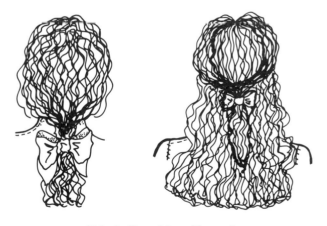

Styles for Bernadette or Marguerite

Method 2
HAND-SEWN YARN HAIR

There are several ways to sew hair on by hand. For example, Felicity's hair (page 97) and elinor's doll's hair (page 57) are little bundles of yarn stitched, one at a time, to her head. Anne of Green Gables (page 139) has strands of yarn sewn using a satin-stitch embroidery technique to cover the back of her head; additional strands at the top and sides of her head are braided to create her hair style.

Style A

The amount of yarn used in this method will vary; however, a skein of yarn will generally be enough to cover any of the dolls' heads in this book. The finer the yarn used, the more bundles you will need to cover the head adequately.

Longer Hair (see Felicity, page 97):

F7 1. Pull a one-yard length of yarn from the skein (do not cut the yarn) and wrap it around three of your fingers five times. Tie the strands in the center with a piece of yarn. Make a total of four of these bundles for the lower edges of the sides and back.

2. Using two fingers and wrapping around five times, make eleven more bundles.

3. Put a spot of glue (either tacky or hot) on the knot of each bundle and place two of the four larger bundles on the right lower side of the face, with the loops of the bundle touching the shoulder. Repeat for the other side. Fill in the lower edge of the back hairline with the other two bundles.

4. Start at the top of the doll's head at the seam and pin the remaining bundles down the seam, until you reach the first large bundle (just below ear level). Repeat for the other side of the head. Pin the remaining bundles on the back of the head, filling in the remaining areas. Spread and re-arrange the bundles, if necessary. Glue them in place.

5. Tie a small bow of 1/8″-wide ribbon and glue it to the side of head, as pictured.

Shorter Hair (See Woman with the Chicken Quilt, page 57):

F8 Depending on the texture of the yarn (thicker yarn will cover more head area), start applying the four larger bundles at ear level. Fill in the remaining area of the head as instructed above.

Style B

F9 Any kind of yarn may be used for this method. Christine Shively used four-ply yarn and split it in half to give a softer and wavier effect (see page 139).

1. On the back of the head, draw a guideline along the neckline.

2. Thread a darning or craft needle with a long length of yarn, at least 4 feet in order to avoid the constant re-threading of the needle.

3. Begin at the top seam of the head and leave a 12″ tail. Each time you refill the needle, leave this 12″ tail. You will use the tails later.

4. Satin stitch (note embroidery diagrams, C8) to fill in the entire back of the head, from one seam to the other.

5. Again using very long lengths of yarn, begin in the center, overlapping the 12″ tails. Loop the lengths of hair 12-15″ out from the head, a fraction of an inch apart. To keep the yarn from bunching up, hold the

finished loops taut in one hand while pulling the new yarn through. Keep long lengths of yarn loose to avoid tangling.

6. When you have reached the desired thickness and have completed half of the face, twist the hair away from the face, not too tightly. Tack it on the side of the head, just below the lip area. Braid the yarn and secure the braid with another piece of yarn. Trim the ends.

7. Repeat this process for the other side of the head.

8. Make small looping stitches on the forehead to make bangs. Keep them loose and fluffy. Loops that are too tight will be a sharp contrast to the rest of the hair.

Method 3
GLAZED YARN HAIR

F10 This method requires no sewing.

1. Glue short strips of yarn to the center front of the head to form bangs. The upper edge of the bangs should overlap the seam at the top of the doll's head.

2. Apply glue to the side of the doll's head and wind yarn onto the head in an oval shape. As you make the oval wider, the yarn will need to be wound only to the top of the neck, but may overlap the top center of the doll's head, covering the upper ends of bangs.

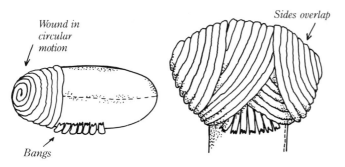

Wound in circular motion

Sides overlap

Bangs

3. Repeat for the other side of the head, beginning the yarn at the center back of the neck to leave a tail. Apply more glue, a little bit at a time, overlapping the wound yarn to build up height.

4. After the hair is in place and the glue is dry, make a hardening mixture of equal parts of water and water-base sealer, or use undiluted acrylic varnish. Paint it on the hair and allow it to dry thoroughly.

Method 4
USING CURLY WOOL CREPE FIBER

Curly wool crepe is effectively used to create doll hair with a lot of wavy curls. Once unbraided, it can also be ironed to straighten the fiber if you want less curl.

F11 Margaret Peters used crepe to create Dirk's hair (page 123). This fiber becomes longer when it is unbraided. She then glued each piece to the center of the head at the part line. The fiber is pulled toward the base of the neck, gathered and tied with a ribbon. You may need to trim the ends.

F12 Becky Tuttle has unbraided 24″ of crepe, pulled it apart slightly to fluff it, and stitched it by hand to her Victorian doll's head (page 17).

1. Pencil the hairline and begin forming loops of crepe approximately 1″ long which almost touch the doll's eyebrows. These loops should be next to each

other and the top of each loop will be tacked into place by using a needle and strong thread.

2. The back of the doll's head will be covered by winding the crepe very loosely in a circular figure. Steps one and two will use all of one package of crepe (12″). Tuck the raw ends under and stitch.

3. Form three large loops at the back of the doll's head. The tops of the loops will be about halfway up the doll's head. The middle loop will be longer than the two side loops, which are about 1/2″ below the doll's shoulders.

4. Wind the rest of the length of crepe into a bun which covers the upper ends of the loops. Continue to hand-stitch crepe in place.

Attach bow

5. Tie a small organdy bow (approximately 1″ wide) and glue it at the top of one of the side loops at the back of the doll's head.

The methods and fibers described above will give your dolls a broad range of hair styles. You will be able to discover many new styles by experimentation. Here are a few styling ideas:

Clockwise from top: Susan Hale, Thomas Gourley, Clinton Gourley, Virginia Avery, Michael Gourley, Miriam Gourley, Helen Pringle

THE BASIC RAG DOLL

The pattern and instructions for this doll are to be used as you wish. I have included many examples of changes to this basic pattern. Shauna Mooney enlarged the pattern at a copy center (page 7); Sally Lampi changed the feet on the ballerina (page 21). Virginia Robertson, Virginia Avery and others created their own clothing for the doll (pages 3 and 21). This doll can be used as a learning tool. Make several and try different methods of making hair, faces and clothing. You will notice the doll doesn't have a face. That is to encourage you to make your own. The following instructions are very general. You should feel completely free to adapt this pattern. The doll may be either a girl or a boy. Although the clothing patterns are also included in Chapter 1, you should read Chapter 2 before you begin the clothing.

BODY ASSEMBLY

Place the fabric right sides together and pin the pattern to the fabric. Follow the directions at A1–F12 for sewing, applying the face, stuffing the doll and applying the hair. (After you stuff the arms almost to the shoulders, top-stitch the shoulder joint as indicated on the pattern, if you wish.)

CLOTHING

Instructions for Pantaloons are given in G1.

Dress

1. Place the pattern on the dress fabric and transfer all markings (see B1).

2. Use your longest machine stitch length to make a gathering stitch from the left front edge of the dress to the tailor tack which marks the black dot.

3. Repeat Step 2 for the right front side and back of dress.

4. Gather the waistline of the dress to the circled dot which is marked on the lower edge of the dress sleeve.

5. Fold the dress skirt up, right sides together with bodice, and stitch from the side edge toward the black dot, starting out with a 1/4″ seam allowance and tapering the seam allowance as you would when sewing a dart.

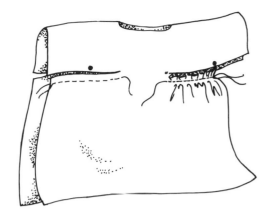

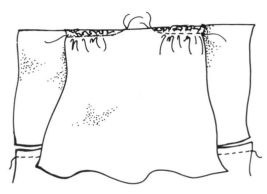

6. Repeat Step 5 for the three other darts and press the seam allowance toward the skirt.

7. Make a slit for the back opening of the dress and clip the lower ends of the slit as designated on the pattern.

8. Cut a bias strip 10″ x 1″. Press under 1/4″ of the long edge. Pull the slit open in a straight line and pin the unfolded edge of the bias strip against the raw edges of the neck slit, with the right sides of the bias strip to the wrong side of the neck slit. Stitch 1/4″ from the raw edges of the slit. Fold the bias strip over the raw edges, with the folded edges of the bias strip covering the previous stitching, and machine stitch it in place.

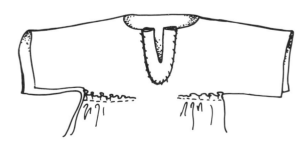

9. Clip the neck edges in the curved areas. Fold under 1/4″ of the remaining bias strip and stitch the strip to the neck edge in the same manner as step 8.

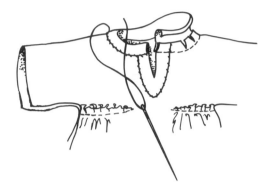

10. Lap the right back neck edge over the left and stitch a snap or button to close the dress.

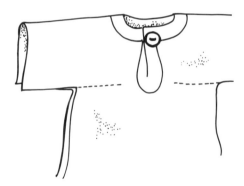

11. Place the dress right sides together, matching the raw edges. Stitch from each sleeve to the bottom hem of the skirt. Clip the fabric where necessary and turn right side out.

12. The dress sleeves and skirt may be hemmed by rolling under a simple narrow handkerchief hem, or lace may be zig zag stitched to the right side of the skirt, the raw edge pressed under, and the skirt hem may be top-stitched close to the lace.

13. The dress may be embellished in any manner you wish. Many ideas will be presented in Chapter 2.

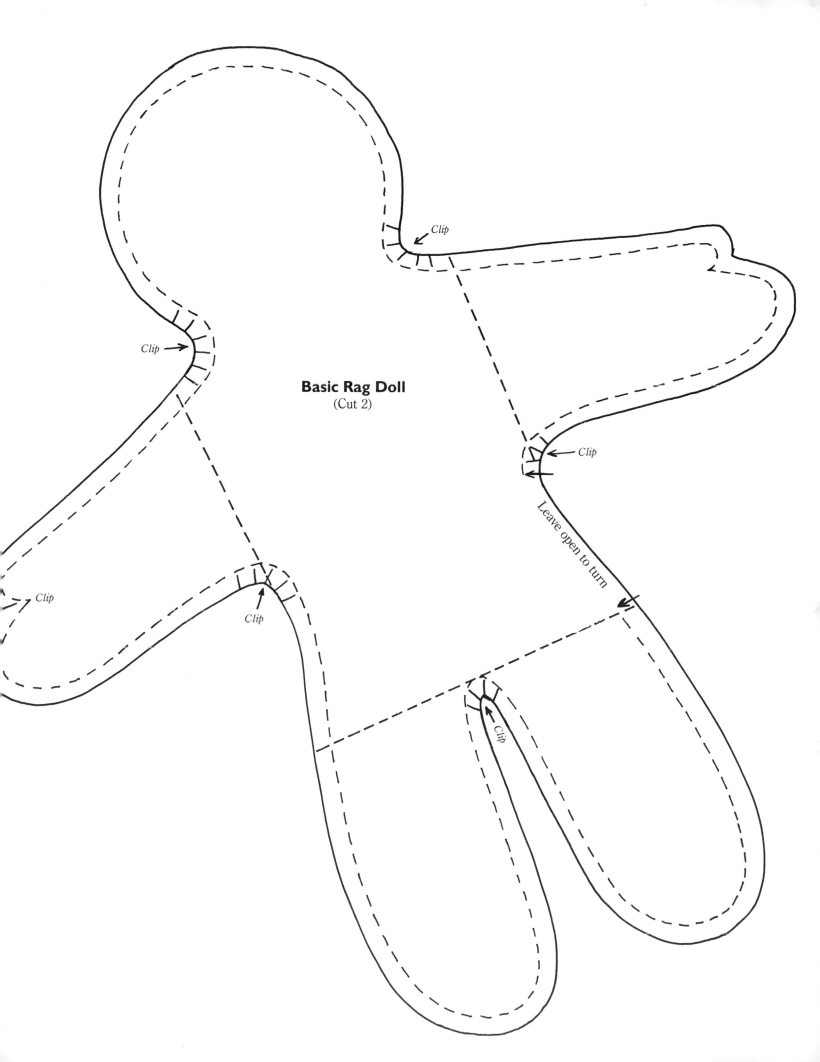

Basic Rag Doll
(Cut 2)

Clip

Clip

Clip

Clip

Clip

Clip

Leave open to turn

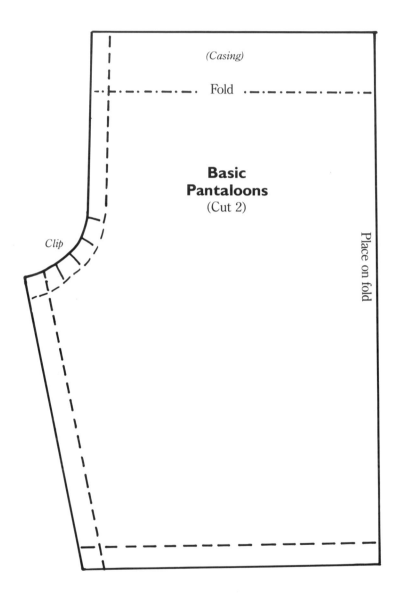

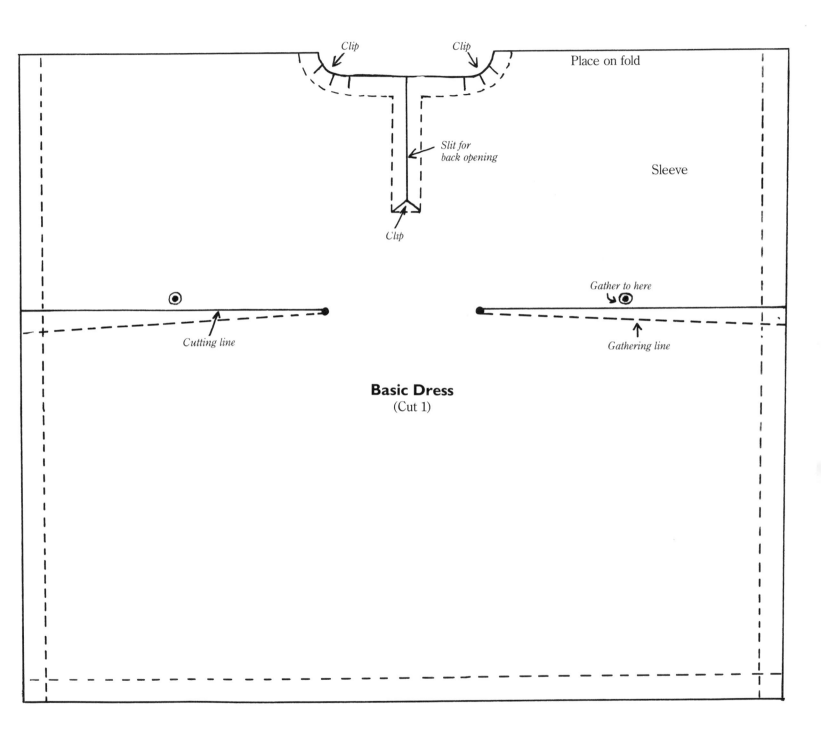

Clip Clip

Place on fold

Slit for
back opening

Sleeve

Clip

Gather to here

Cutting line

Gathering line

Basic Dress
(Cut 1)

Chapter 2
DOLL CLOTHING

A cloth doll's personality is developed by two main details—facial features and clothing. Many times, when I hear people discussing particular dolls, they include detailed descriptions of what the doll was wearing. We have often heard the saying "Clothes make the woman." I believe that clothing also makes the doll.

Cloth, like nature, has a variety of surface textures and colors. These are important factors to consider when constructing a doll. Texture and colors can be an important way of communicating a mood. A piece of burlap may evoke feelings of a rustic country mood, while velvet connotes richness. Muslin may symbolize rural, peasant or practical ideas, while a beautiful paisley print may remind us of a lovely Victorian shawl. elinor peace bailey's black doll is wearing African prints, indicating not only elinor's exciting color sense but her respect for other cultures.

The selection of color is also an important aspect in creating the doll clothing. Color choices communicate emotions. Blue may symbolize loyalty, sadness or cold, while yellow makes one think of cheerful, sunny days. Combinations of colors also portray the personality of the designer. A designer who makes use of bold primary colors makes a different statement from one who uses delicate pastels.

There are many styles of fabric—prints, solids, checks, plaids, florals, paisleys, etc.—and most can be used for doll clothing. If a print (or plaid, floral, paisley, etc.) is used, it should be appropriate for the size of the doll. For example, a large cabbage-rose design would probably not be the right scale for the clothing of a 12" doll. Prints may be mixed. If you are unsure of how to select appropriate prints that enhance each other, pick one main print that appeals to you. Look carefully at the colors and select other prints that have some of the same colors. Solids may be mixed in with very good results.

Cotton prints are very popular in dollmaking, but one should not overlook silk and metallic fabrics, such as lamé. If lamé is used, it should be lined, as it frays easily. Finish all the raw edges of silks and lamé by serging or zig zagging to prevent unraveling. Hand-dyed fabrics may also be used. I have already discussed various painting techniques in Chapter 1, but here are a few other painting techniques as they pertain specifically to embellishing fabric for doll clothing.

Fabric manipulation is another exciting aspect of dollmaking. When you dye, paint or change the texture of fabric, either by quilting, pleating or some other method, you are creating a new piece of fabric which is unique. For example, notice Margot Strand-Jensen's version of the

Basic Rag Doll (page 21), which has hand-printed leaf designs.

Children may also create clothing for dolls by using simple sewing methods. You can teach a child to use a needle and thread to hand-gather a strip of tulle or other fabric into a skirt. (Make sure the thread is strong enough to endure this learning process.) You may want to stitch it onto some kind of simple waistband—perhaps a ribbon which can tie in a bow at the back. This is a good method for beginners, especially if you are teaching them to sew for the first time. If they are too young or not interested in sewing clothes, you can let them use fabrics that have less of a tendency to ravel, such as knits or felt. Children can cut out clothing items and glue or hand stitch them in place. You will notice that the Batman doll (page 32) is of one-piece construction in black fabric, with painted facial details. An emblem from a cereal box is glued to his chest and he is wearing a black cape cut from cotton knit. You might also let children create painted clothing.

Other methods of embellishment include the use of ribbon work, appliqué, beading and quilting. Adding glittery accents is sometimes an interesting embellishment. You will note the gold stars used as part of Miss Liberty's costume (page 32) as a good example of this. Buttons may also be used decoratively.

This chapter will include basic construction guides, everything from setting in sleeves to making a binding for a coat such as the one worn by the Woman with the Chicken Quilt (page 57) by elinor peace bailey. Some of the garments are very simple. Some, such as those worn by the Princess Bride (page 65), are elaborate and time-consuming. I think there is something here for everyone.

First, clear away all the scraps, hair fibers and stuffing from where you have created your doll body. Assemble an assortment of fabric and trims. Soon, you will discover the combination the doll wants you to use. Get ready for an exciting adventure!

TOOLS AND SUPPLIES FOR CONSTRUCTING CLOTHING

Basic Sewing Kit   (See Chapter 1, "Tools and Supplies")

An Assortment of Fabric
Cotton prints
Cotton solids
Velvets
Silk
Ethnic fabrics
Metallic fabrics

Trims
Fusible webbing (paper-backed)
Cotton batting
Cording
Ribbon (wired, silk, taffeta, antique, etc.)
Beads (glass, wooden, ceramic, etc.)
Tulle (available in many colors)
Lace (wide, narrow, antique, tea-dyed, colored, white, etc.)
Box for old laces
Silk and/or paper flowers, ribbon roses, etc.
Dried flowers
Buttons (antique, rhinestone, pastels, all sizes)
Straw hats (various styles, sizes)
Stiff art paper (for crown)
Doll-size chains, necklaces, etc.
Rayon and metallic machine embroidery thread
Miscellaneous items, such as rayon tassels, braid, etc.

Additional Tools
Razor knife
Needle board (for pressing velvet)
Narrow floral wire
Wire nippers
Small pliers

Additional Painting Supplies
(Note: Many of the products listed in Chapter 1 will be utilized when decorating fabric for clothing.)
Solid stick paint (oil-base)
Marbleizing equipment (water-thickener, eyedroppers, acrylic paints, cake pan, wide-tooth comb)
Resist-dyeing equipment (resist, fabric paints)

SELECTING FABRIC

When selecting fabric, you should consider several key points:

COLOR

Color provides emotional as well as intellectual stimuli. Color can tell us when a peach is ripe, but it can also give us the information of a green traffic light. It can be used to create a mood, such as a blue stage light for the feeling of mystery. When selecting the colors of fabric for a doll, we should ask ourselves what feeling we wish to create and whether the doll will be a focal point or a decoration in a room.

Visual aspects of color include HUE (the color itself), VALUE (dark/light quality), and INTENSITY (its degree of brightness or purity). In addition there are warm and cool colors. Warm colors generally involve the red-to-yellow family; however, blue may be added to warm colors to change them. Blueish-red is a cool red. Cool colors, such as those in the blue-green family, may be warmed by having a little orange added to them. Cool colors usually recede, or are less noticeable, while warm colors advance and make a louder statement. Intense colors also seem to advance, while grayed colors (those that are dulled by either the opposite color in the color wheel or by the addition of black) seem to recede.

HARMONY

Harmony is achieved by consistency of fabrics or materials, the overall line of the doll, form and textures. However, one should not confuse harmony with an exaggerated concern for matching everything. A sense of excitement may be created by vitality as well as by a certain unpredictability; the piece can still be harmonious.

TEXTURE

Texture includes much more than something soft and furry. Texture is surface quality, whether it exists or is implied by various printing techniques. Texture in fabric has great variety, from rough fabrics such as burlap, bouclé or loosely woven linen or wool to smooth silk, tightly woven polished cotton or some of the synthetic fibers, such as acetate or polyester.

Texture may also be created by the manipulation of fabrics. For example, fabric can be quilted traditionally with batting between two layers of cloth, or trapunto, which gives much more texture and definition to the quilting. Fabric may be gathered in tiny folds, tied with strings and tie-dyed by dipping it in several colors. Silk may be permanently crinkled by twisting it while it is damp, placing it in a light-weight muslin bag to prevent scorching and drying it at medium heat.

When selecting fabric, you must think about how it will hang or drape, how it will look when stuffed or sculpted, and whether the texture will enhance the final effect of the piece. The process used to produce the fabric is an important consideration. Woven fabrics are made from vertical warp yarns that are interwoven with horizontal weft yarns. This process enables the weaver to produce a great variety of textures simply by using a variety of textured yarns. Knitted fabrics have a lengthwise rib created by the knit stitch. The greatest degree of stretch is across the rib pattern, whereas the greatest degree of stretch in woven fabric is the 45-degree or bias angle. Felted (fused) fabrics are made of fibers that are interlocked by pressure, beating, moisture and heat, the oldest method of making cloth. True felt is made from wool fibers, sometimes combined with fur or hair; it can be stretched or molded over a form, but most kinds are not very strong or durable.

FABRIC TYPES

There are many types of fabric, most of which may be used in dollmaking. Natural fibers, such as cotton and linen, come from plants; wool and silk come from animals. Synthetic fibers include rayon, acrylic, nylon, acetate and polyester. Each has distinct properties:

Fabric Types	Description
Cotton	Most commonly used fiber. Comes in many different weights, strengths and textures. Can be washed and dried. Easily dyed and bleached. Must be ironed.
Linen	One of the strongest natural fibers. Great variety, from a very rough texture to very sheer. More soil- and moisture-resistant than cotton. May be washed or dry-cleaned.
Wool	Takes dye well, but damaged by bleach. Least expensive of all animal fibers. Very resilient. Limited range of weights and finishes, but often blended with other fibers. Some wool blends are washable and can be pressed with a pressing cloth. All pure wool should be dry-cleaned. Susceptible to moth damage, but many wools are pre-treated against moths.
Silk	Produced by the caterpillar of the domesticated moth *Bombyx mori*. Available in a number of textures and weights. Very resilient and strong. Fairly expensive, but a good choice for dollmaking because of its durability and variety. Hand-washable with mild soap. Takes dye well. Only hydrogen peroxide or sodium perborate bleaches should be used.
Acrylic	Crease-resistant and heat-sensitive. Often blended with wool; the blend is washable. May mold or shape to some degree while still warm from ironing.
Nylon	Incredibly strong, elastic and dirt-resistant. When blended with other fibers, produces fabrics with those qualities. Produced in a variety of weights. Should be ironed on the wrong side with very low temperature setting.
Polyester	The most springy, resilient and wrinkle-resistant of all fibers. Often

blended with natural fibers. Batting and sewing threads are often produced from polyester and cotton. Polyester blends are washable and not harmed by chlorine bleach. Dry quickly.

FABRIC MANIPULATION

FABRIC PAINTING

Fabric Preparation

Whether or not you plan to wash the fabric later, pre-wash anything you are going to paint. This helps the fibers to absorb color. Pre-wash with soap, not detergent, and hang the fabric to dry; then press it.

Paint Supplies

Some of the painting supplies and techniques were discussed in Chapter 1. Here I will focus on fabric embellishment for clothing. Painting for embellishment can be done using acrylic paints or any of the oil-base solid stick-paints, which can be used by stenciling or placing an object under the fabric to make a rubbing.

Resist Dyeing

Originally developed for silk painting, resist dyeing has a very long history. All resists act as a barrier to keep paint or dye from flowing beyond its line into another color. There are several kinds of resist, including wax, gutta (used with dyes) as well as resists for use with acrylic paints. Resist is a colorless medium applied to outline an area. Resist may also be brushed onto fabric for an outline or to create an abstract design.

The advantage in using a resist which is compatible with acrylic paints is that it is "user-friendly." To create a design using acrylic fabric paint, use the resist to outline the areas you wish to paint and let it dry 30-45 minutes. Your paint should be diluted according to the instructions in Chapter 1, C4, Step 1, and applied to the enclosed areas. When the dye is completely dry, it should be heat-set. To remove the resist, soak the fabric in cool to lukewarm water, or wash it in the machine on gentle cycle. Remove to the dryer set at medium heat.

Gutta and wax, on the other hand, require more study and expertise. I recommend taking classes or researching these two methods before attempting them. The dyes used with gutta are a little more difficult to work with than acrylic paints. Wax is not only difficult to apply (first melted, then applied from a cone applicator with a tiny hole), but

difficult and messy to remove.

Marbleizing Fabric

One of the easiest methods of marbleizing fabric is with the use of a powder concentrate called MarbleThix. When you mix the prescribed amount of powder in a cake pan full of water and leave it overnight, the water becomes the texture of runny gelatin. Eyedroppers are used to drop a mixture of acrylic paint and water onto the surface of the thickened water. Any number and combination of colors may be used. You then swirl the solution with a large comb or hair pick to create patterns with the paint. A piece of plain fabric is placed on the surface of the mixture for five seconds and then hung to dry. The paint on the surface will have been transferred to the fabric. By adding new paint colors, you can use the thickener over and over. The procedure is simple enough for children to enjoy.

After Painting

Heat-set dyes before adding embellishing paints, such as glitter paints. When the fabric dyes are dry, place a press cloth over the painted area and set with an iron at medium heat for at least ten seconds. You can also set the dyes by turning the garment inside out and placing it in a dryer at medium heat for ten minutes. This is especially important if you are creating a special T-shirt to match a doll you are making for a child.

Do's and Don'ts of Washing

DO be sure to let all paint cure for at least five days before washing. This is very important! DON'T use detergents. They are designed to remove anything, including paint. DO wash in *cold* water using a *mild* soap. You may hand wash or turn the garment inside out and machine wash (gentle cycle). DO place it in the dryer for ten minutes to fluff the fibers. Remove and hang it to complete the drying process. If necessary, press clothes on the wrong side.

OTHER EMBELLISHMENTS

In addition to fabric painting, surface texture and color may be enhanced or created by using embroidery floss, by itself or mixed with blending filaments which give a metallic sparkle to the floss. Note embroidery stitches diagram at C8.

Beading

Beading is also a popular embellishment, with glass, ceramic or wooden beads. elinor peace bailey even used a bead for the eye of the chicken on the quilt her doll is holding. When you work with small glass beads, the most

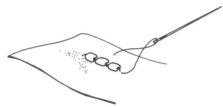

difficult job can be threading the needle, since beading needles are very thin. In this case, a special needle threader may be used. Needle sizes 9-12 are suitable for most beadwork. Thread the needle with double sewing silk, nylon thread or thin crochet yarn. Rub the thread across beeswax for added strength.

There are many types of beading, including weaving, stringing and stitching directly to fabric. It is the latter type of beading that will be most often used in dollmaking. One type of direct beading is called overlaid stitching or Sumatra stitching. It is a technique of sewing on strings of beads. You need two needles and two double threads of sewing silk. Thread one of these with beads; use the other to sew the rows of beads across the first thread with small stitches.

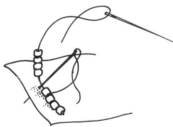

Another method of sewing directly to fabric is embroidery. Beads can be stitched to fabric either singly or in groups. If you are sewing just one bead, it should be large enough to stand out as a point of focus. The most suitable stitch is a tacking stitch. Choose a bead with a large hole, such as a ring bead, and attach it with several stitches (six is about right). The stitching then becomes part of the decoration. Groups of beads may also be stitched on individually but placed very close to one another. Afterwards, thread a strand of cotton through all the beads so they lie in the same direction.

Cross-locked beads are a single strand of beads which have been strung together with several interwoven strands of thread. They may be stitched to fabric either by hand or by machine. To stitch by machine, draw a line on the fabric where the beads are to be attached. Use a zipper foot and zig zag the strand of beads to the fabric. The zipper foot will rest next to the beads as you stitch.

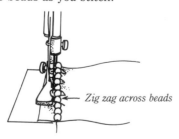

Zig zag across beads

Laces, Trims and Buttons

Antique laces and various trims such as cording, ribbon and fringe may also be used in embellishing doll clothing. Old or interesting buttons can be wonderful embellishments. Just remember the scale of the doll and don't overwhelm it with buttons which are too large. A button can also be used as a brooch or earring.

Embellishing with Ribbon

Ribbons may be used as embellishment, either by stitching them onto fabric, thereby creating a new fabric pattern, or by folding, tying bows or making ribbon roses which are attached on the outside of doll clothing. To apply ribbon directly to fabric, top-stitch close to each side of the ribbon or machine embroider along the edges of the ribbon. If you machine embroider, use paper underneath (typing paper may be used) to keep the fabric from puckering. If a straight stitch is used, stitch as close to the edges of the ribbon as possible. You may also wish to use decorative machine embroidery stitches to apply the ribbon to fabric.

Decorative Ribbon Art

Loops of 1/4"-wide satin ribbon may be used as a base for a ribbon rose or other embellishment. Loop the ribbon back and forth in varied lengths. Attach a wire in the middle, twist and clip with a wire cutter. Bend the sharp ends in toward the middle of the loop.

A ribbon or lace fan may be used as the base for a doll-size nosegay or embellishment on a hat. I made this type of embellishment on Marguerite's hat (page 107). To make the fan, fold the lace in half and gather it at the base, near the raw edges. Twist floral wire around to secure it. Clip the wire near the base and bend the sharp ends in toward the fan.

Ribbon roses may be purchased or made. Commercially made roses may be spray-painted with gold paint, brushed with glitter or pearl paints or highlighted with a wash (C4) in a complementary color.

To make your own ribbon roses requires patience and a great deal of practice, so practice on inexpensive ribbon before attempting the more expensive wire-edged or metallic ribbons. Depending on the size you need, use 3/4" or 1-1/4" ribbon. The length of ribbon will depend on how large you want the rose, so do not cut the ribbon; just unwind some from the spool.

1. Cut the ribbon end diagonally.
2. Make a double pleat, parallel to the diagonal end.

3. Wind ribbon around the pleat several times to form the stem and center of the rose.

4. Turn the ribbon away from you at a 45-degree angle. Continue wrapping ribbon around the stem until you reach the end of the angle.

5. Make a new 45-degree angle each time you come to the end of the previous angle. In this way you begin to form the petals. When the rose is large enough, softly gather the ribbon at the base and wrap floral wire tightly around the base to secure it. (Use small pliers.) Take a needle and matching thread and stitch through the base of the rose, through as many layers as possible to keep it from unraveling. Wrap the thread around the base and tie a knot.

Clip the stem close to the base of the rose if you will be gluing the rose on a hat or lapel. If you are making a small bouquet, do not clip the stem: leave long wires at the stem and wrap them with floral tape.

You can create ribbon bows to ornament doll hair or clothing in several different ways. Below are two methods:

Small Single Bow

1. Cut a piece of 1/2″ ribbon 1-1/2″ to 2″ long.
2. Tie a knot in the center. This should be rather loose.
3. Clip the ends in an inverted V pattern, as illustrated.

4. Glue it in place.

Traditional Bow

1. Cut a length of ribbon about three times longer than the width of the finished bow plus three to four extra inches for the knot.
2. Form two loops and tie them together.
3. Adjust the loops—smaller by pulling the ends of ribbon or larger by pulling slightly on the loops.
4. You may need to pull the knot tighter after adjusting the bow.
5. Trim the ends at a diagonal or with inverted V's.

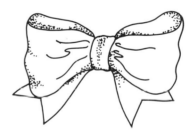

COSTUMED CLOTHING

Many contemporary cloth dollmakers prefer to research the clothing they make. There are many books written about costuming. When you go to your library, you might look under the following headings: theatrical costumes, specific clothing or fashion illustrators, such as Erté or George Barbier, history of costume or a specific kind of costume, such as gypsy or Amish.

A few years ago, I was visiting Lebanon, Ohio, and was in a picturesque inn, looking at the ways the various rooms were decorated in period furniture. I was especially charmed by the simplicity and beauty of the Shaker furniture and was inspired to create an authentically dressed Shaker doll. I went to the local university library and looked up Shakerism. I read several volumes on the subject, including Shaker textiles, furniture-making and the history of Shakerism. I wanted to create clothing for the doll which was typical of the type worn by Shaker women in 1850. I made sketches from photographs, read all I could find and eventually finished the clothing for the doll. I even made one doll that was dressed in winter clothing and one that was dressed in a summer costume. I enjoyed creating those dolls more than any other and, when I look at them, the memories of the initial inspiration and the subsequent research still warm my heart.

I feel this book would not be complete if there weren't a costumed doll. Karen Balding has created such a doll, using an illustration from a fourteenth-century manuscript as her inspiration. She read the accompanying story to get a feel for the character, which is a very important part of costuming. The details of the costume are exquisite—from the beautiful red silk surcote to the white fur plastron—and I hope she will inspire you to find your own area of interest and create your own historically costumed doll.

HOW TO MAKE PIPING

Piping can be an appropriate trim for doll clothing. When you go to the fabric store to purchase the cording for the piping, keep the size of the doll's clothing in mind. The bigger the piping is, the more difficult it will be to insert in the seams of the doll's clothing. The smallest cording will be appropriate for most of the doll's clothing. You may want to trim the edges of the quilted jacket (G7) with piping, or insert piping to finish the edges of Felicity's quilt, rather than use the traditional binding. Piping will make a nice accent at the bottom of a skirt hem or down the front of a doll's coat. To make piping, follow the steps listed below:

1. If the piping is to go around small curves, you may want to cut the strips of fabric on the diagonal, but for most straight edges, you may cut strips of fabric on the straight grain. Cut the strips of fabric 3/4″ wide and as long as you want.

2. Fold the fabric around the cord, with the right side of the fabric on the outside, and stitch along the edge of the cord using your sewing machine zipper foot.

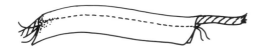

3. If the piping is to go around curves, clip the piping every 1/4″.

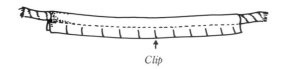

Clip

4. Place the raw edge of the piping on the raw edge of the fabric and baste it in place, using your zipper foot.

5. Place a second layer of fabric against the first piece of fabric, with the right sides together and the piping sandwiched in between, and stitch next to the cording. Turn the fabric right side out and press. Or, if you are stitching piping on a quilt to finish the edges, do Step 4, then turn the raw edges inside the quilt. Fold under the backing and pin to the piping, covering the raw edges. Hand stitch the backing to the piping.

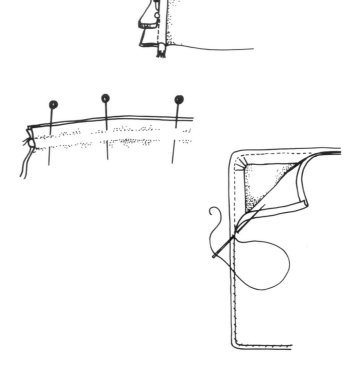

ATTACHING BINDING TO CLOTHING

Occasionally, you will need to bind the edges of a neck or skirt opening. The opening may be created by a small perpendicular slit from the neckline downward or by a back center seam that is not stitched to the top. Binding may also be used to cover the raw edges of a quilt or the edges of a doll's coat.

To cut binding for doll clothing or accessories, measure around the area you need to bind, and use that as the length of the binding. The width may vary, depending on how much of the edge the binding is to cover, but for most doll clothing 1-1/4″ wide will be right. To apply the binding:

1. Press under 1/4″ along the sides of the entire length of binding.

2. Pin the right side of the binding to the right side of the quilt or garment with the raw edges together. (The back opening of the Basic Rag Doll's dress, on page 33, was finished using a similar method.)

3. Stitch 1/4″ away from the raw edges and clip if it is necessary.

4. Fold the binding over to the wrong side, with the pressed edge of the binding just covering the previous line of stitching. Hand stitch the binding to the garment and press it. If you wish, you can machine stitch the binding to the wrong side (Step 2), fold it over to the right side and top-stitch it by machine (Step 4).

CLOTHING CONSTRUCTION

PANTALOONS

GI   1. Fold the fabric right sides together and pin the pattern to the fabric. Cut out the fabric.

2. If you choose, you may cut the pantaloons from lace, such as the batiste lace used on Becky Tuttle's Victorian doll (page 149). You can place the pattern with the leg opening on a scalloped edge of wide lace to avoid having to hem the leg opening.

3. If you are not using lace but something like tea-dyed muslin, as on Roxanne Becker's Mary Ruth (page 87), hold up the pattern to the doll body and decide how long you want the pantaloons. They may go to the ankle or just below the knee. Allow 1/2″ for hemming, and cut the pattern out.

4. (A) If the pattern includes a fold in the center front of pantaloons like Rebecca Ann's (page 131), place the front and back of the pantaloons with the right sides together and stitch the side seams. Press them open and finish the lower edges of pantaloons using one of the methods below. Place the pantaloons together with the right sides together and stitch the crotch seam. Clip the curves and press the seams.

(B) Mary Ruth's (Felicity's and Anne's are also similar) pantaloons are cut with the side of the pantaloons placed on the fold. Before you stitch any seams, finish the lower edges using one of the methods below. After the edges are finished, place pantaloons with the right sides together and stitch the crotch seams. Clip the curves and press the seams open. Fold the pantaloons in half with the right sides together, matching the seams, and stitch the inseam of the legs.

(C) Becky Tuttle's Spring Promenade (page 149) has not been cut on the fold, but the bottoms of the legs are cut on the lace border. Place the pantaloons with the right sides together. Stitch the crotch seam, clip the curves and press the seams open. Place the front and back with the right sides together and stitch the inseam and the side seams.

5. (A) If you wish the lower edge of the pantaloon leg to be gathered, turn the bottom of each leg under 3/8″. Stitch a 1/4″ seam to form a casing. Insert an embroidery-floss drawstring through each casing, using a long blunt craft needle.

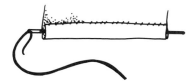

(B) Attach 1″-wide flat eyelet lace or other lace to the bottom of each leg opening by pressing under 1/4″ of the bottom edge and top-stitching it over the raw edge of the lace.

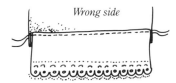

Wrong side

(C) If you want the pantaloons to look fancier, sew an additional trim between the bottom casing and the eyelet for a ribbon to be laced through.

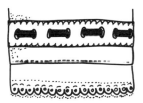

(D) Zig zag the raw edges, press up 1/2″ and sew a gathering stitch along the zig zagged edge. Pull the thread to gather it slightly and top-stitch to secure the gathers.

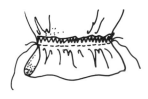

6. Make a top casing by pressing under 1/8″ or zig zagging the edge to finish. Fold the top edge of the pantaloons under about 1/4″ and stitch next to the edge of the casing. Leave an opening so you can insert the elastic.

7. Feed elastic through the casing and stitch it together. Ribbon or embroidery floss may be used as drawstrings to fit pantaloons to the doll. If you prefer this to elastic, after the pantaloon is finished make a small slit in the front seam in the casing and feed through embroidery floss or ribbon with a blunt craft needle.

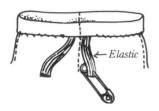

← *Elastic*

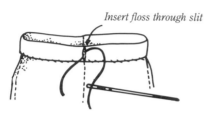

Insert floss through slit

PETTICOAT

 1. Press under 1/4″ of the bottom edge. The petticoat will be a rectangular piece of fabric. The bottom edge will be one of the longer edges. As with pantaloons, if you desire to use batiste lace to avoid having to hem or finish the lower edge with additional lace, cut out a rectangular petticoat with the raw edge at the top. The shorter edges will form the back seam.

2. Sew the center back seam. Press it open.

3. Press under 1/8″ or zig zag the edge, fold it over 1/4″ and stitch close to the edge to form a casing.

4. Insert drawstrings as for pantaloons (Step 7 above).

DRESS

Fold the fabric right sides together and pin the pattern pieces to the fabric. Cut as indicated and transfer all markings. Follow the directions for the specific style of dress, as indicated below:

Dress with Set-in Sleeves

G3 The instructions for each doll's clothing will indicate what steps you will need to follow:

1. Sew the shoulder seams and press them open. Stay-stitch around the neckline 1/4″ from the edge. Clip the curves.

2. (A) Fold the bias strip in half lengthwise. Pin the raw edges of the bias strip to the neck edge with the raw edges together and sew it. Press the raw edges toward the dress and top-stitch.

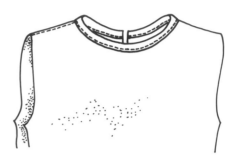

—OR—

(B) Use gathered lace instead of bias tape. Just place the gathered lace with the neck edge of the bodice, right sides together, and stitch the lace to the neck. Clip the curves and top-stitch the neck edge on the outside.

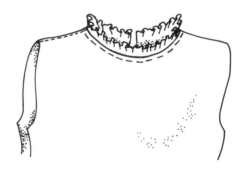

(C) Instead of bias strip for the finished neck edge, some patterns may call for a facing or a lining. Stitch the shoulder seams of the facing and press them open. Place the facing and bodice right sides together, matching the seams and the neck opening. Stitch around the neck opening as indicated on the pattern. Clip curves, turn right side out and press. Tack the facing to the seams, if necessary.

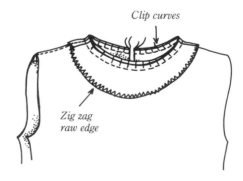

Clip curves

Zig zag raw edge

3. Gather sleeves at the top edge. (Note: Various patterns may indicate gathering between notches, etc.)

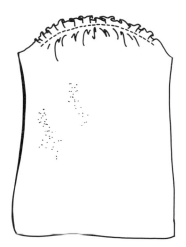

4. (A) Finish the lower edges of the sleeves by rolling under a simple hem or by using any of the methods at G1: Step 5A (casing), 5B (eyelet or lace edge), 5C (additional trims) or 5D (gathered hemmed edge).

(B) You may want to sew a cap sleeve on the dress, like the one worn under the jacket of Professor Holly Beetle (page 115). Cap sleeves are not pre-gathered.

8. If the dress skirt doesn't have any seams other than the back center seam (one-piece construction), stitch the underarm seams of the bodice.

9. Machine stitch a gathering stitch along the top edge of the skirt (or a ruffle) and pull to fit the bodice.

10. Place the bodice and gathered skirt right sides together and stitch the skirt to the bodice. (You may wish to do a two-layer skirt like the one worn by Professor Holly Beetle on page 115.)

11. Stitch the center back seam from the lower edge, stopping 2-1/2″ below the gathered skirt. Press the seams open. If the dress has double skirts, stitch one skirt at a time.

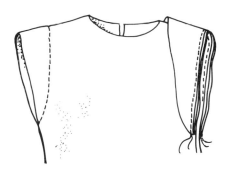

5. Place the gathered sleeve and bodice with the right sides together and stitch them together. Press the raw edges toward the bodice. If the skirt is of one-piece construction, go to Step 8.

6. Gather the skirt sections to fit the bodice. Pin the gathered skirt to the bodice, right sides together, and stitch it.

7. Place the dress right sides together and stitch the side seams from the wrist to the hem of the skirt. Sew the center back seam. Press the seams open.

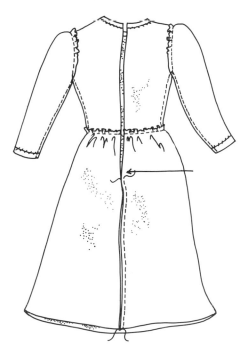

12. Turn up the hem for the lower edge of the skirt and press it. Turn under 1/4″ of the raw edge and blind stitch by machine or by hand, or edge with binding.

13. If you wish to make a tuck in the skirt, turn the hemline to the inside of the dress 3″ all the way around. Measure and press a little at a time.

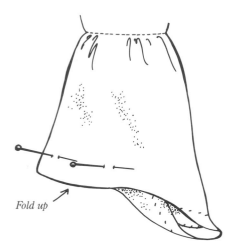

Fold up

14. Stitch 1/2″ from the folded edge. Press the tuck toward the bottom hem. Anne of Green Gables' dress (page 139) has two of these tucks, about 1/2″ from each other. If you wish, you can stitch a row of lace under the bottom tuck.

Alternate Finishing Techniques

15. Roll under a small handkerchief hem and machine stitch; press. If the neckline gaps (for bias neckline only), insert a floss drawstring through the bias at the neck and pull it to fit the neck. Tie a bow in back.

Or press under 1/4″ of the back dress opening and place the dress on the doll. Lap the right edge over the left and hand stitch the opening closed; or, you may sew buttons on the left side and buttonholes on the right side, if you prefer to make the dress removable.

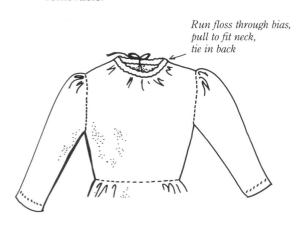

Run floss through bias, pull to fit neck, tie in back

Gathered Bodice

G4 This variation of the bodice above is Mary Ruth's best dress (page 87).

16. Sew the shoulder seams of the bodice and press them open. Sew a gathering stitch at the neckline and bottom of the bodice front, as shown. Gather them to the length indicated. Place them on the doll to ensure a good fit.

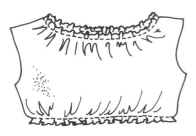

17. Top-stitch over the gathering with a narrow stitch to hold it in place.

18. Sew three rows of gathering stitches on the caps of sleeves. Gather the cap to fit the armhole. Top-stitch over the gathering to hold it.

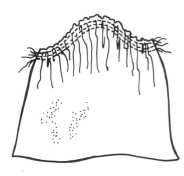

19. Sew four rows of gathering stitches on the skirt front and back. Gather the skirt front to 5″ and each skirt back to 2-3/4″ wide.

20. Sew the bodice front to the skirt front, the bodice back to the skirt backs, as directed above in Step 6.

21. Gather the wrist end of each sleeve (with three rows of stitching) to fit the doll's arm loosely. Lightly gather 1″-wide lace and top-stitch it to the end of each sleeve (see G1, Step 5B).

One-Piece T-Shaped Dress or Blouse

G5 1. Place the dress front and dress back right sides together and stitch the shoulder seams.

2. Place the facing front and facing back right sides together and stitch the shoulder seams. Press all seams open.

3. Zig zag the raw edges of the sleeve opening and along the outer edges of facing. Place the dress and

facings right side together, matching any seams and notches included in the pattern.

4. Stitch along the neck edges and front edges of the facing or neck opening. (You will notice that Bernadette's and Marguerite's facing and blouse fronts do not match. The extra fabric on the blouse front serves as a front facing for the blouse.) Zig zag along the edges to finish them. Clip the corners, curves, etc. and trim the seams allowance on the neck edge to 1/8".

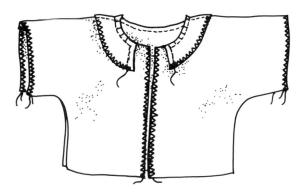

5. Stitch the side seams and clip the curves.

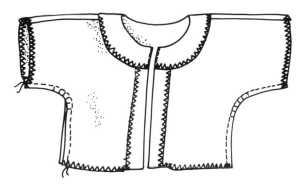

6. For the dress, turn it right side out and press.

7. For the blouse, fold the front facing, right sides together, and stitch 1/4" from the lower hemline.

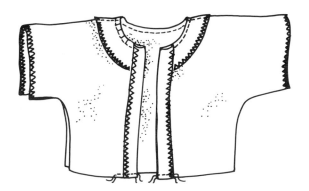

8. Roll under a double hem on the sleeves, if desired, and machine or hand stitch it.

9. Zig zag along the lower edge of the blouse or dress to finish the raw edges. (The blouse has been folded and stitched at the lower front corners, so you will need to turn the corners wrong side out and stitch through both layers of fabric.)

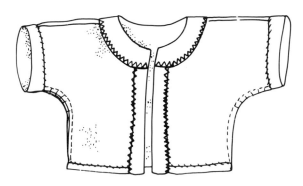

10. Roll up the hem for the dress or blouse and hand stitch or machine stitch it in place.

11. Make three buttonholes on the right side of the blouse. Sew buttons on the left.

Doll Skirt

G6 1. Press under 1/4" of the long edge of the waistband. Gather the top edge of the skirt to the desired width. Bernadette's and Marguerite's skirts should be gathered to 6-3/4".

2. Press under 1/4" of the skirt sides from the upper gathered edge to the dot. Clip to the dot.

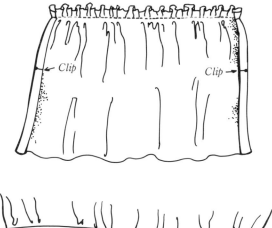

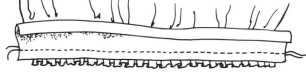

3. Pin the skirt to the waistband, right sides together, matching the raw edges. The waistband will be 1/2" longer at each end.

4. Stitch the skirt to the waistband as illustrated.

5. Fold under 1/4″ of each end of the waistband. Fold the waistband over the raw edges to cover the stitching. Tack the waistband to the back of the skirt by hand.

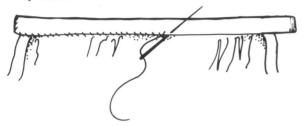

6. Stitch the back seam up to the dot. Press the seam open. Zig zag the lower raw edge of the skirt to finish the raw edge.

7. Fold on the hemline and blind stitch.

8. Pin antique lace (about 1-1/2″ wide) under the bottom edge of the skirt on the wrong side. Overlap the lace at the back of the skirt and stitch them together. Stitch the lace to the lower edge of the skirt, using small stitches. Try not to let the stitches show on the right side of the skirt. Press the skirt.

9. Place the skirt on the doll and overlap the waistband. Hand stitch it in place.

QUILTED JACKET OR COAT

G7 1. Cut out the jacket and lining pieces. If you desire a lined jacket with no quilting, eliminate Steps 2-4. Place the jacket right sides together and stitch the shoulder seams, pressing toward the back. Repeat for the lining.

2. Cut a 20″ square of cotton/polyester batting (very thin) and pull it apart to make the batting even

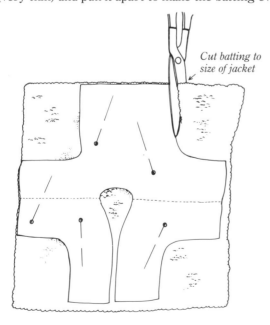

Cut batting to size of jacket

thinner. Place the bonded side of the batting on your work surface. Pin the jacket, right side up, onto the batting. Trim away excess batting.

3. Machine quilt the jacket directly onto the batting. Do not use lining underneath. The bonded side of the batting should be directly on the feed dogs. I used metallic thread to quilt, but rayon thread is also beautiful. When using specialty threads, decrease the upper tension on your machine and increase the stitch length to at least 10 stitches per inch. If the thread breaks, decrease the tension a little more and increase the stitch length slightly. Use white cotton/polyester bobbin thread. If you are using a Bernina machine, thread the bobbin thread through the small outside hole on the bobbin. Quilt in channel or grid patterns, as illustrated.

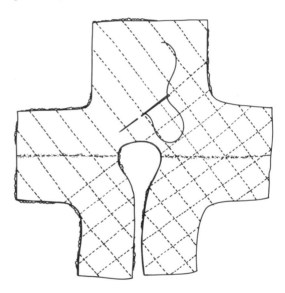

4. Hand bead, if you desire. For example, you can stitch one bead in the center of each grid pattern.

5. Stitch the side seams and clip the curves. Repeat for the lining. Press the seams.

6. Do not press the right side of the fabric if you have used metallic thread, as it may melt.

7. Pin the jacket and lining right sides together, matching the seams and the raw edges. This would be a good time to insert piping around the front and neck edges of the jacket, if you wish. Stitch around the bottom, front and neck edges, leaving a 2″ opening at the back center of the lower jacket edge for turning.

8. Clip curves and corners, then turn the jacket right side out. Turn the sleeve edges of the jacket and lining inside, toward the batting, so raw edges don't show. You may bind the sleeves with contrasting fabric by using the same method used to bind the neck of the dress (page 44). Or, turn in the raw edges of the

jacket sleeves and lining sleeves and hand stitch them together. If you wish, small cording may be stitched around the ends of the sleeves as an accent. Press the sleeve edges on the wrong side, turn them right side out and roll the cuff up about 1″. Place the jacket on the doll and open the jacket to form lapels, as illustrated.

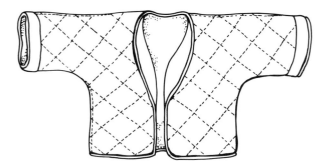

9. To hold the jacket closed, make a sash for the waist from sparkly tulle (worn by Marguerite) or gold rope cording (worn by Bernadette, page 107). The tulle is 6″ wide by about 24″ long. Tie the tulle into a bow at the front side. The cording is approximately 14″ long. Knot the ends of the cording before tying it around the doll's waist.

PIECED JACKET

G8 1. Cut various strips of co-ordinating fabrics for a strip-pieced jacket. Do strip piecing on cotton batting or flannel which is 30″ × 7″.

2. Starting with a triangle at a corner, pin it in place, right side up. With the right sides together, lay

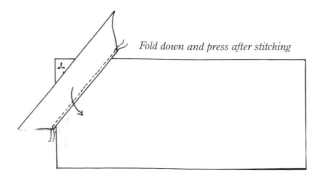

Fold down and press after stitching

your first strip at the edge of the triangle and stitch it in place, as illustrated.

Allow the strip to overlap at the edge so the fabric will cover the batting. Turn, press and trim it. Repeat the process until all the batting is covered. There is no prescribed width for the strips. Cut them as wide or narrow as you prefer.

3. Place the lining at the back of the stripped piece. Cut three 45″ lengths of 1-1/2″-wide strips for the jacket binding and one 8″ strip on the bias for the neck binding. (When the binding is for curved pieces, it *must* be cut on the bias.)

4. Cut a slash up the center of the jacket front and cut out the neck. Both the lining and stripped piece should be pinned together.

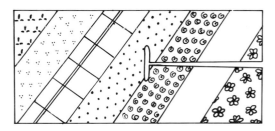

5. Cut binding strips into:
   Two 10″ pieces for the armhole
   Two 15″ pieces for the center front
   Two 5″ pieces for the front hem
   One 9″ piece for the back hem
   Four 5″ pieces for the kick-pleat strips.

6. Press under 1/4″ along the edges of all binding pieces. Place the binding and edge of jacket lining right sides together. In order to prevent puckering, stitch the binding to the lining, going in one direction; when you fold the binding over to top-stitch, stitch in the opposite direction.

7. Attach the binding in the following order (see diagram):
   Center front
   Arm holes
   Four lower side edges of coat
   Bottom edges of coat.

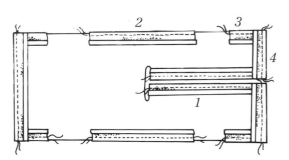

8. Fold the jacket right sides together, matching the lower edges. Stitch a 1/2″ wide seam from the edge of the armhole binding to the lower sides of the coat, stitching through the coat front and batting only. Do not stitch the lining in this seam. It will be stitched later. Clip as indicated in the diagram, and trim the seam allowance.

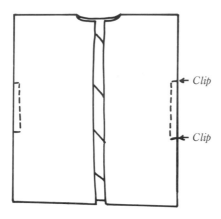

9. Fold the lining over, raw edges tucked inside, and hand stitch it closed.

PINAFORE

G9 Pinafores for Anne of Green Gables (page 139) and Mary Ruth (page 87) have lined bodices. Anne's has lace and tucks, too. Here are directions for a doll's pinafore:

1. Place the fabric right sides together and cut 1 bodice front, 1 bodice front lining, 2 bodice backs, 2 bodice back linings, 1 skirt and 1 pocket (for Mary Ruth only).

2. Place the bodice front lining and bodice back lining pieces right sides together and stitch them at the shoulder seams. Press them open.

3. For Anne's pinafore, pin 2″-wide lace down the center front of the bodice front rectangle. Machine or hand stitch it in place.

4. With the wrong sides of the bodice together, fold 1/2″ from one edge of the lace. Press. Stitch 3/8″ from the folded edge, forming a tuck. Press away from the lace. Repeat for the other side of the lace.

5. Insert 3/8″-wide to 1/2″-wide lace just under the folded edge of the tuck and machine stitch it.

6. Fold 1/2″ from the scalloped outer edge of the lace. Make another tuck, just as you have above.

7. Baste the last tuck 3/8″ from the folded edge. Trim excess fabric 1/8″ from the basting stitch.

8. Center the lace and tucks on the front bodice and pin it in place. Stitch along the basting line, stitching tucks and lace to the front bodice. Trim the fabric to match the bodice front.

9. Stitch the shoulder seams of the bodice front and back pieces as for the lining.

10. Place the bodice and lining right sides together. Stitch around the neckline, center backs

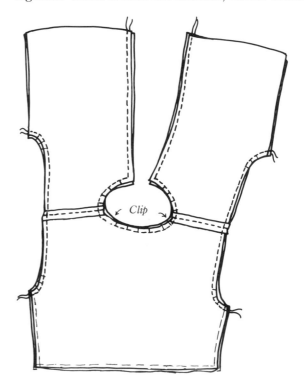

and armholes. Clip the curves, turn the right side out and press it.

11. Place the raw edges of the underarm sides right sides together, matching the armhole seams.

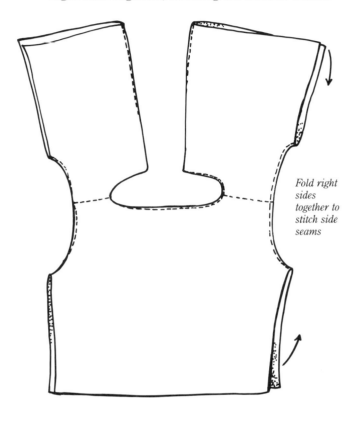

Fold right sides together to stitch side seams

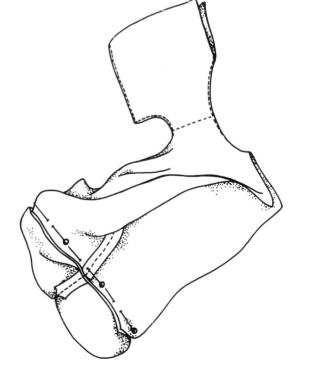

Stitch the side seams, starting at the bodice and ending at the lining. Press them open. The bodice is now ready for you to insert the skirt.

12. Pockets (optional): Zig zag along the top edge of the pocket and fold the top edge over 1/4″ with the right sides together. Stitch the sides 1/4″ from each edge.

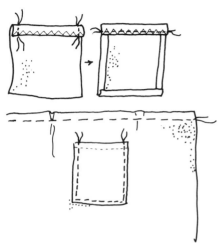

13. Press under the remaining three sides of the pocket 1/4″ and stitch the top close to the zig zagged edge. Pin the pocket at the center front of the pinafore skirt and top-stitch it to the apron.

14. Turn under a handkerchief hem at the center back edge of each side of the skirt for Mary Ruth; make a 1″ hem for Anne. Hem the bottom edge of the skirt and blind stitch it.

15. Stitch 5/8″-wide lace 1/2″ above the folded hem of the skirt. Make two 1/2″ tucks. The lower tuck should just cover the stitching at the top of the lace. The upper tuck should be 1/2″ away from the stitching of the lower tuck.

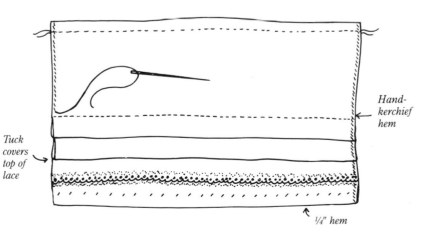

Hand-kerchief hem

Tuck covers top of lace

1/4″ hem

16. Stitch a machine gathering stitch at the top edge of the pinafore skirt and gather it to fit the bodice. Mary Ruth's pinafore has two additional rows of decorative gathers. If you like this, stitch two additional rows of gathering stitches 1/4″ from each other. Place the skirt right sides together with the bodice and stitch it. Fold up 1/4″ of the bodice lining and hand stitch, covering all raw edges of the skirt.

17. Top-stitch close to the edge around the neckline, waistline and armholes, if you wish.

18. Overlap the back edges of the dress and hand stitch it closed. Stitch on beads to simulate buttons, or use actual buttons.

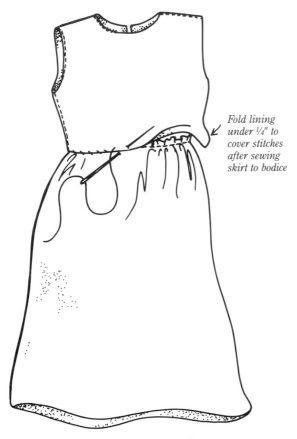

Fold lining under ¼″ to cover stitches after sewing skirt to bodice

Chapter 3
THE DOLLS

The process of selecting dollmakers for this book was difficult, since there are so many talented designers. Rather than making a list of people, I began by choosing the types of dolls I wanted to include. I listed them in the following categories: Victorian (lace, silk ribbons and pastel colors), old-fashioned (very traditional, using materials that might have been available to a dollmaker 100 years ago), little girl (a doll that might be made for a special child), whimsical (a doll dressed in old-fashioned clothing made from unexpected combinations, such as velvet and cotton, showing a sense of humor), arty (non-traditional decorative doll), romantic (combination of Victorian, art deco and 1920's, with modern touches), patriotic (red, white and blue), country (for the antique collector and country fans), storybook (a favorite character from a novel) and fairy-tale (a romantic or fantasy character).

From that point, my job was much easier. I could almost immediately think of dollmakers who fit most of these categories. I contacted each of them, gave them a few guidelines and let them work on the designs. After the sketches were approved, we all got down to business looking for fabrics, cutting out patterns, stitching, stuffing, embroidering, painting and assembling instructions. Several of the dollmakers expressed their reluctance to let these new creations leave home. I understood how they felt, when I received the boxes and lifted each wonderful fabric-encased personality out of the tissue and packing chips. To the dollmakers, I express my gratitude for the long hours, for their dedication to this project and for their friendship.

Arty

WOMAN WITH THE CHICKEN QUILT

by elinor peace bailey

Elinor was raised in Scarsdale, New York. She attended Tyler School of Fine Arts at Temple University and Brigham Young University, where she earned a B.S. degree in art education. She has also studied at Parsons School of Design, the Art Students' League and San Jose State University.

She lives in Hayward, California, in the San Francisco Bay area, where she is the mother of nine children. In addition to this noteworthy career, she has designed and published numerous patterns including her Victorian doll pattern, which was my first introduction to her designs.

elinor is not shy about proclaiming the merits of making cloth dolls. In her new book, *Mother Plays With Dolls*, she urges her readers to get rid of the notion that when creating dolls one has to perform to others' expectations. She urges others to free themselves creatively, and her work speaks well of her ability to experiment freely.

She is also the designer of numerous doll-embellished items of clothing. One of the first garments she made was a beautiful quilted coat of aqua polished cotton covered with imported lace, bits and pieces of acquired trims and loaded with dolls. Some were hidden, but most were easily visible. She tells about the dream from which this coat evolved: the coat was constructed using the colors and embellishments she remembered from the dream.

elinor is a champion of women everywhere. Her creations speak to everyone, even though many do not understand her language completely. elinor is not shy about controversy, yet she has a warm and tender heart. All of these qualities are portrayed in her work.

This doll is called Woman with the Chicken Quilt. She writes: "Most dolls are white. Ethnicity is an issue in doll making. An opportunity to use the wonderful African fabrics and make a woman of African descent comes along seldom. So I picked up my scissors and made her. Not a 'mammie' doll or some other offensive stereotype, but an African woman who loves her heritage and quilts."

MATERIALS LIST

(Use 100% cotton throughout)
5/8 yard of flesh-colored fabric for body
1/4 yard of muslin for underwear and socks
1/8 yard of black or brown fabric for shoes
Scrap of dark peach for mouth
3/8 yard for dress
1/4 yard for belt
1/4 yard for lining of jacket
1/4 yard of flannel or thin cotton batting for inner lining
1/8 yard each of 4 co-ordinated fabrics for strip-pieced jacket
1/4 yard each of 3 fabrics for background, border and back of chicken quilt
1/4 yard of cotton batting for quilt
4 scraps for chicken
12 oz. bag of stuffing fiber
1/4 yard of lace for underwear
1/8 yard for binding of jacket
Blue Sharpie (blue fine-tip permanent-ink marking pen)
White fabric paint (for eyes)
"Bittersweet" crayon
Paper-backed fusible webbing for chicken quilt
Yarn for hair (something with "personality")

CONSTRUCTION

1. Cut the head and nose from flesh-colored fabric.
2. Cut the mouth from peach fabric.
3. Follow directions at B2.
4. Stitch the head together following directions at E3 (Steps 1-3), and stitch the nose and mouth according to instructions at D1.
5. Paint the facial features, starting with the whites of the eye. Color the eyeball and the lids with the Sharpie pen. Rouge in the cheeks with a "Bittersweet" crayon. Refer to C6.

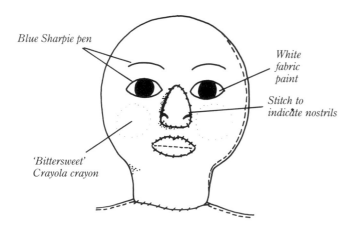

Blue Sharpie pen

White fabric paint

Stitch to indicate nostrils

'Bittersweet' Crayola crayon

Body and Legs

1. Cut both the body and the legs from the flesh-colored fabric. Cut the appliqués (undergarments and socks) from the selected fabrics.
2. Apply the appliqués, following the pattern for placement (see D3). Apply the lace over the raw edge of the underwear on the leg. Stitch it in place.
3. Stitch the legs and the body, then insert the head (see E13).
4. Partially stuff the hand and top-stitch the fingers (see E5, Step B). After stuffing the hand, needle sculpt to form a wrist (see E8).
5. Attach the legs to the body (see E15).

Hair

See the hair instructions at F7 (Step 1) and make 12-14 bundles, then continue at F8.

Dress and Sash

The dress is made according to the directions at G5, Steps 1-6 and 8-10. Place the dress on the doll, lap the right side of the opening over the left side, and close it with several stitches. Make the sash as follows:

With the right sides of the fabric together, fold the sash lengthwise. Stitch around the raw edges, leaving an opening at the center for turning. Turn the sash, stitch the opening closed and press it. Now dress that woman and tie on her sash!

Coat

See the pieced jacket instructions at G8.

Quilt

1. Using a scrap of fusible webbing, trace the chicken body, chicken beak, tail feathers and chicken feet separately. Use a pencil to transfer the design onto the paper side of the webbing. Cut each part out in a square format. (For example, cut out a 2″ × 3″ piece of the webbing onto which the feet have been traced.) Iron the webbing to the wrong side of the chosen fabric. The paper side will *not* be next to the fabric. Follow the directions given on the webbing to ensure good bonding. Cut out the various chicken body parts and remove the paper backing.
2. Apply the chicken body, beak, tail feathers and feet to the quilt. Appliqué around all parts of the chicken with a satin zig zag stitch, as instructed at D3.
3. Use a rotary cutter to cut the borders and place the right sides of the border and the quilt top together. Stitch along the raw edges, then press them toward the border. Repeat this step for the top and the bottom edges.

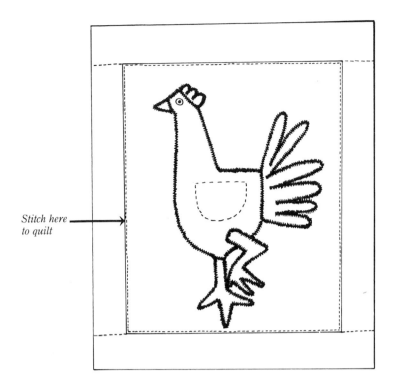

Stitch here to quilt

4. Stitch on a bead or two for the chicken's eye.

5. Place the quilt top right sides together with the fabric selected for the quilt back. Pin it in place, then cut out the quilt back. Cut a piece of cotton batting the same size as the quilt top.

6. Pin the quilt top and back right sides together with the batting underneath, matching the outside edges. Stitch around the outer edge, leaving an opening for turning. Trim the seam allowance to 1/8″.

7. Turn and press the quilt, then stitch the opening closed.

8. You may wish to quilt this or put a needle in the doll's hand so she can stitch it. She'll love it!

Finishing Touches

This woman will also demand a pair of earrings (buttons or hand-made from Sculpey®) and a quilt basket to stash her chocolate.

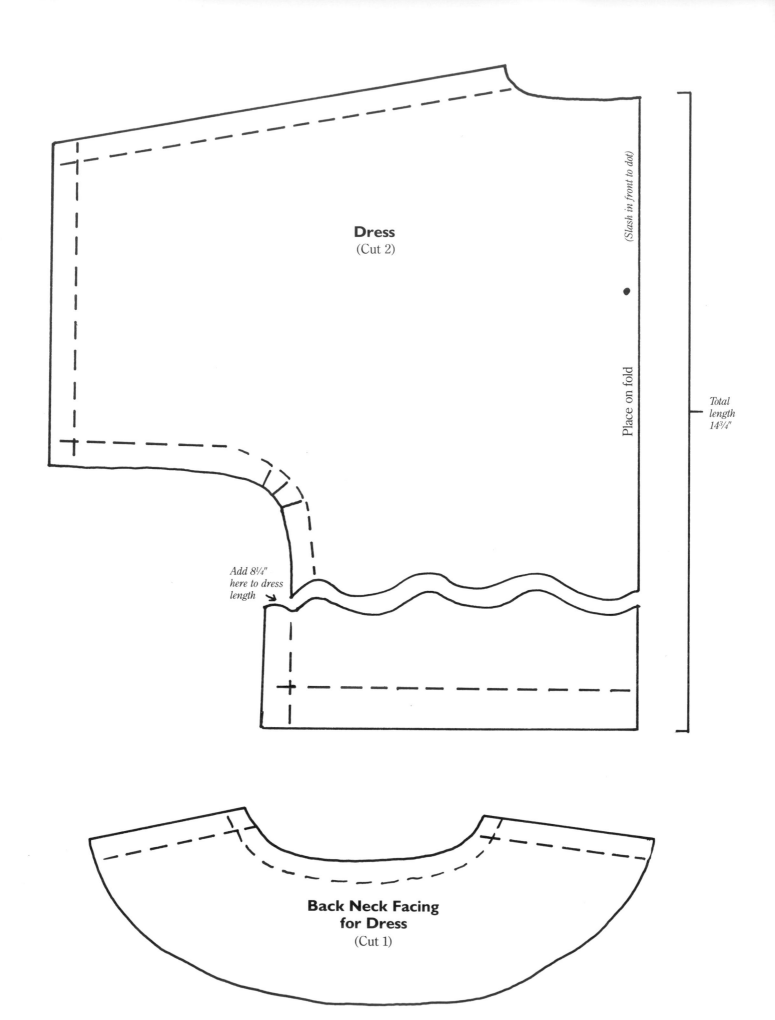

Dress
(Cut 2)

(Slash in front to dot)

Place on fold

Total length 14³⁄₄"

Add 8¹⁄₄" here to dress length

Back Neck Facing for Dress
(Cut 1)

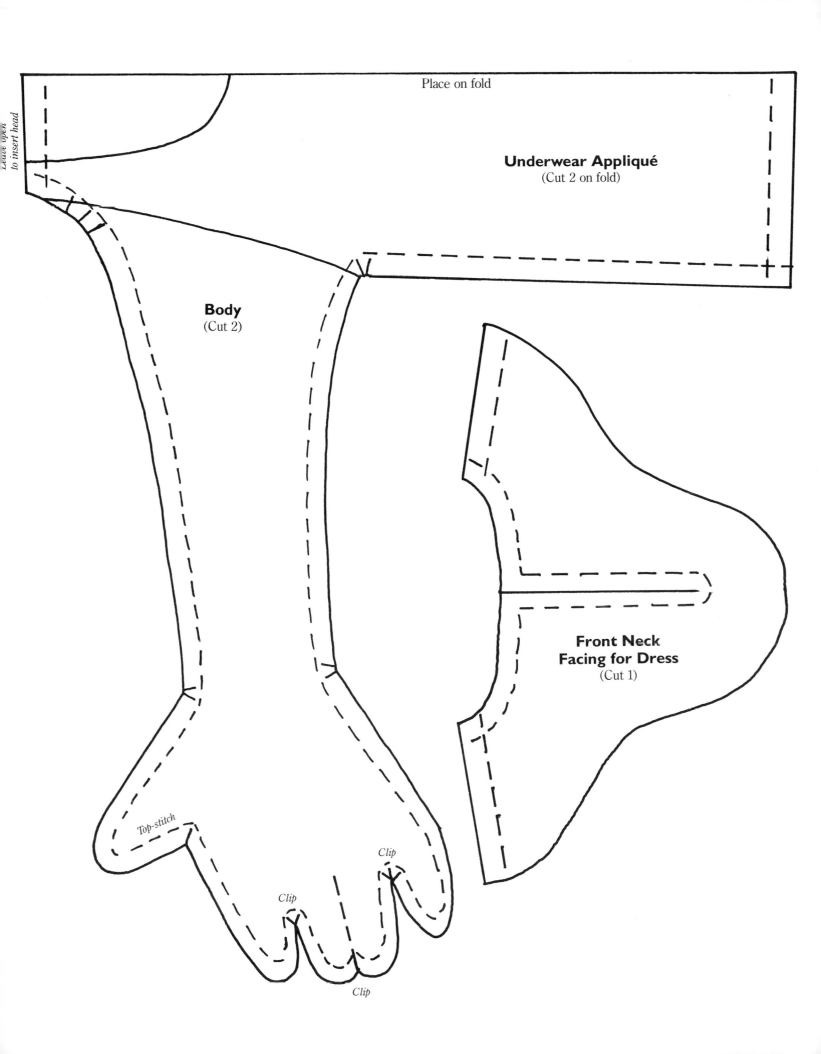

Place on fold

Leave open
to insert head

Underwear Appliqué
(Cut 2 on fold)

Body
(Cut 2)

**Front Neck
Facing for Dress**
(Cut 1)

Top-stitch

Clip

Clip

Clip

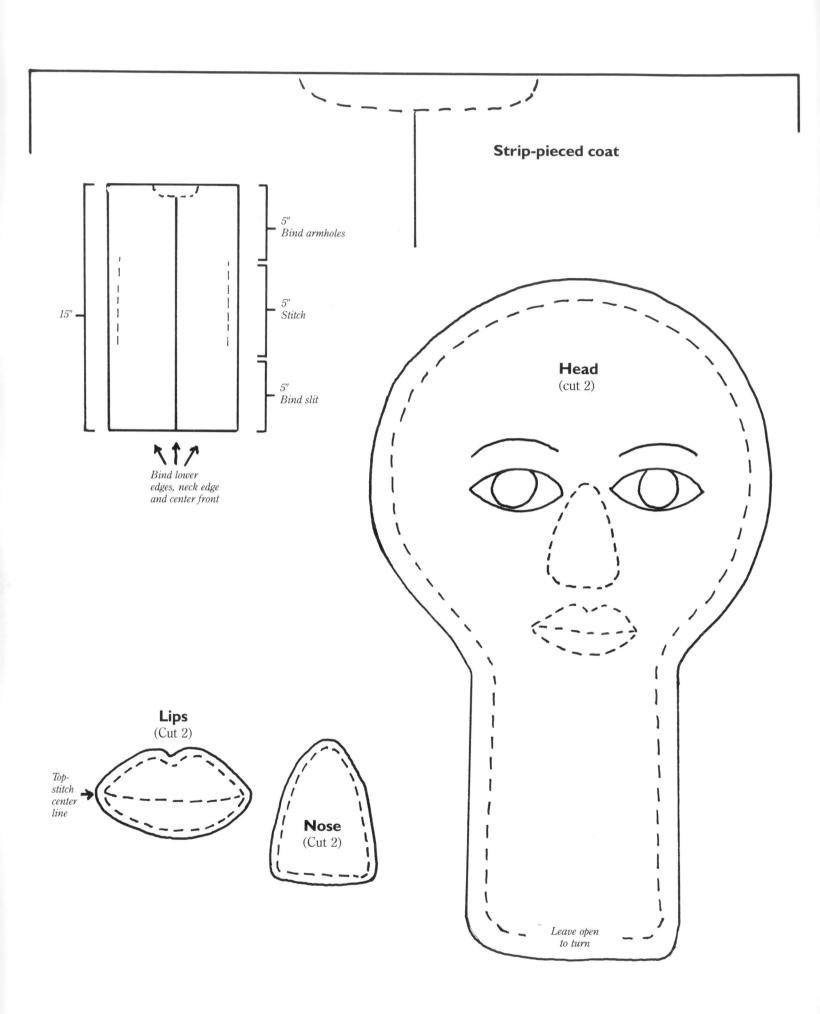

Strip-pieced coat

5"
Bind armholes

5"
Stitch

5"
Bind slit

15"

*Bind lower
edges, neck edge
and center front*

Head
(cut 2)

Lips
(Cut 2)

*Top-
stitch
center
line*

Nose
(Cut 2)

*Leave open
to turn*

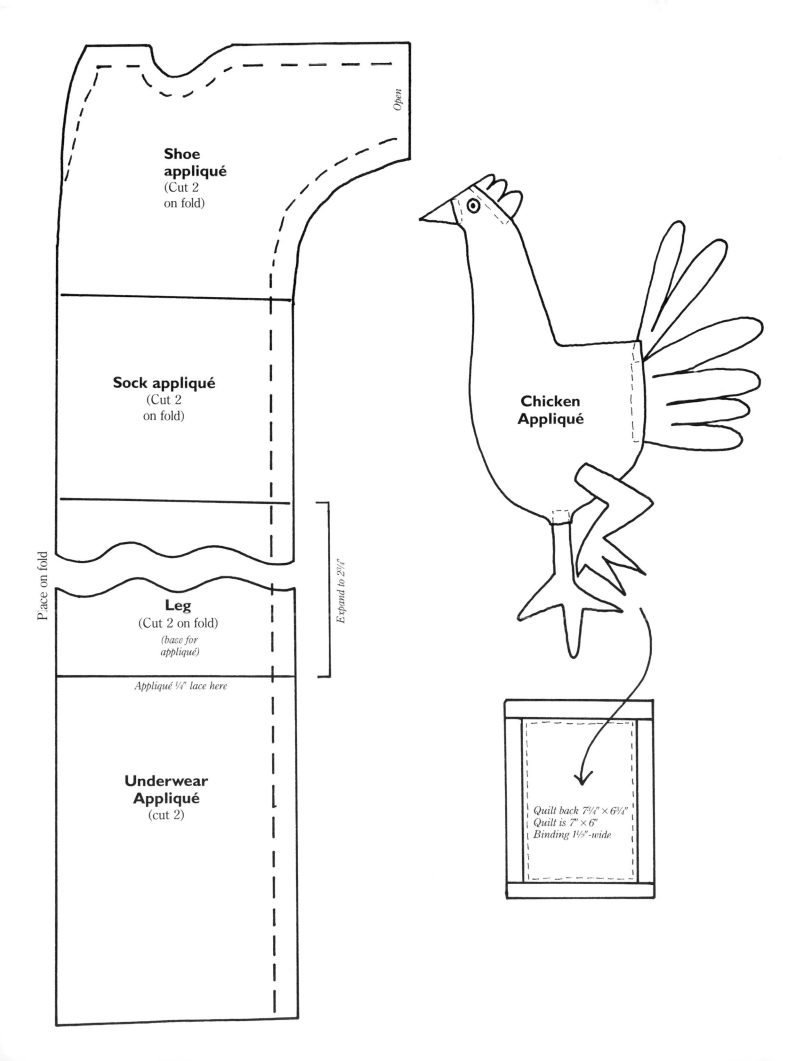

**Shoe
appliqué**
(Cut 2
on fold)

Open

Sock appliqué
(Cut 2
on fold)

Place on fold

Expand to 2¾"

Leg
(Cut 2 on fold)
*(base for
appliqué)*

Appliqué ¼" lace here

**Underwear
Appliqué**
(cut 2)

**Chicken
Appliqué**

Quilt back 7¾" × 6¾"
Quilt is 7" × 6"
Binding 1½"-wide

Fairy-tale
THE PRINCESS BRIDE

by Karen Balding

Karen began thinking about dollmaking while she was driving a bus. She wanted to make dolls to give to two of her smaller passengers, so she purchased a commercial pattern. As she began this project, she decided to change the face a little, then she thought the legs should be a little longer. With this experiment, she found the challenge very exciting and decided to create her own patterns. She began by designing dolls and dressing them in nineteenth-century costumes. According to Karen, the clothing became the most exciting part of dollmaking; she made many trips to the library to research historical costumes.

When I asked her what she thought the most difficult aspect of dollmaking was, she was surprised at how much work was required to stuff a doll correctly, the great care but also the amount of strength required.

The Princess Bride is a good example of Karen's love for costumes. She describes the costume:

"Our princess is dressed in red, a favorite bridal color in olden days.

"The cotehardie, or underdress, in red silk has sleeves embroidered with gold flowers. The red velveteen surcote, or sideless gown, has jeweled buttons, and the neck is edged in black velvet. The small formal train befits the occasion.

"She wears the long flowing hair of maidenhood; after her marriage it will be concealed within the headdress. This 'crowning glory' has a horned cap edged in black and covered with a net of gold cords, surmounted with a roll of red silk. Her noble blood entitles her to wear a crown above it all. A heavy gold chain lies on her neck, and gold and white pointed shoes finish the costume. A betrothal ring is seen on the first finger of her right hand.

"The object of everyone's admiration, she modestly casts her eyes down. Holding the folds of her skirt in one hand, she steps forward to greet her prince."

Karen's inspiration for this doll came from a fifteenth-century illustrated manuscript, *Renaud de Montauban*. Clarrise is the daughter of King Yon.

MATERIALS LIST

Doll Body

1/3 yard of fine-textured 100% cotton bleached or unbleached muslin for the body

Stuffing

Fabric paints: coral, Indian green, antique white, spice brown, white, black and colorless paint medium

Powder blush

Synthetic hair

Rit® dye: rose pink and tangerine

#2 lead pencil

Cotehardie (the undergown)

1/2 yard of red silk

1/2 yard of lining

Gold embroidery thread

Silk thread (to close the back opening)

Surcote (the sideless gown)

1/2 yard of red velveteen

White rabbit fur

White silk lining

Plastron base fabric (muslin)

Medieval-looking buttons

1 yard of 3/16" or 1/4" wide black velvet ribbon

Horned Headdress

Buckram

Smooth double-knit fabric

Black velvet ribbon (3/16" or 1/4" wide)

Gold wire mesh ribbon

Gold enamel spray paint

Padded Roll

Red silk fabric

25 gold-plated beads

Blue glass jewel

Sculpey® or other clay which may be cured at a low temperature

Crown

Heavyweight art paper, such as bristol board

Gold spray paint

14 wooden beads (5 mm.)

13 white stones

Glass jewel to match the headdress

Shoes

Gold-colored leather

Narrow gold cord

Tacky glue

CONSTRUCTION

Doll Body

1. (Optional) Tint the fabric according to the directions at A1.

2. Trace the face, hands, arms and feet onto the fabric, according to the instructions at B1 and B4.

3. Paint the face using the tip of a toothpick. Carefully trace the eyes with medium-brown paint. With a #00 brush, fill in the white area of the eyes with white paint. Paint the iris with green paint and the pupil with black paint. Add a pinpoint dot of white paint in the right side of each pupil for highlight. Use the small brush to trace the contours (the eyelid crease, along the nose, around the nostrils and on the chin) with a mixture of spice brown and antique white, thinned with textile medium or fabric paint fixative. Use the toothpick to trace the eye contours (eyelid crease and the crease just below the eyes) and the nostril area with light brown. Use the brush to paint the eyebrows the same light color as the hair (warm golden brown). Paint delicate sculpted lips: a dark brown center line, the lips themselves applied with coral fabric paint thinned with textile medium. Apply a very slightly colored wash under the eyebrows and on the eyelids.

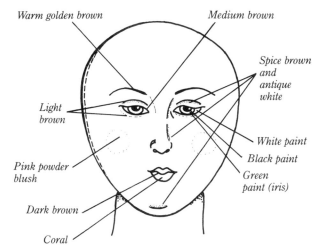

Warm golden brown — Medium brown — Spice brown and antique white — Light brown — White paint — Black paint — Green paint (iris) — Pink powder blush — Dark brown — Coral

4. Follow the instructions at B2 and B3 for the torso and E3 to stitch all the body parts together. Use small machine stitch lengths (15-20 stitches per inch for the body and 30-35 stitches per inch for the hands).

5. Stuff the hands according to the instructions at E4. Shape the hands and arms while you are stuffing them. Bend the fingers down while stuffing and bend the right wrist up. Hand stitch a dart at the top side of the wrist to help hold its shape. Continue stuffing the arm and bend it at the elbow, making a dart on the top side of the arm and hand stitching it to pull the forearm close to the body.

6. Stuff all the body parts and attach the head according to the instructions at E12.

7. Attach the arms and legs to the torso according to the directions at E17.

8. Construct a wig for the doll according to the directions at F6, Steps 1-8 and 11.

9. Apply pink powder blush to the doll's cheeks.

Cotehardie

1. Trace the sleeve pattern onto the silk, make tailor tacks, and transfer the embroidery designs, noting instructions at B3 and B5. Embroider the sleeves using a back-stitch with gold thread; then cut out the sleeves. Stitch the darts for the elbow (to accommodate the bent arm more easily). Stitch the gown together according to instructions given at G3 (Steps 1, 3, 5 and 8). Repeat these steps to sew the lining.

2. Since the cotehardie has no separate skirt, place the dress and lining with the wrong sides together, fold under 1/4" of all the sleeve and sleeve lining hems, the skirt and lining hems, and the neck and back openings. Pin them together and hand stitch all the folded edges together.

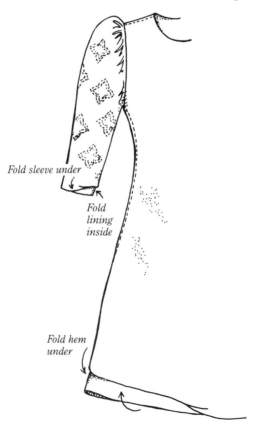

Fold sleeve under

Fold lining inside

Fold hem under

3. Dress the doll by putting her feet through the neck opening. Carefully ease the dress up the doll's body and insert the right arm into the sleeve. Slowly work the sleeve up the arm. Put the left arm into the sleeve and close the back opening by lacing with a needle and silk threads. Tie the threads at the top of the dress.

Surcote

1. Place the train and skirt with the right sides together and stitch the side seams. If you are using velvet, press the seams open on a needle board (which will prevent the velvet pile from being flattened). Leave one of the side seams open above the dot indicated on the pattern. Bind the opening with silk, according to directions on page 44.

2. Cut out the surcote base front and back, place them with the right sides together and stitch the shoulder seams. Baste the back of the base to the end of the left side piece. Press the shoulder seams open and pin the skirt to the center front of the surcote base. Make a large box pleat in the front center of the skirt and small box pleats around the rest of the skirt, and pin the pleats to the surcote base. Hand stitch the base and the skirt together.

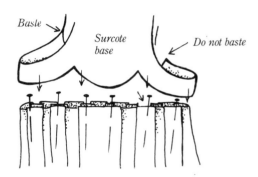

Baste

Surcote base

Do not baste

3. Cut out the surcote base lining pattern (front and back). Place the right sides together and stitch at the shoulder seams. Press open and place a thin bead of tacky glue on the outer edges of the surcote base. Place the wrong side of the silk lining on the underside of the base and wrap the lining edges around the base to glue them in place. Clip the edges where it is necessary. The right side of the lining is now on the inside of the garment. (See the illustration at Step 6.)

4. Place the patterns on the back (*not* the fur side) of the rabbit pelt with the fur growing downward.

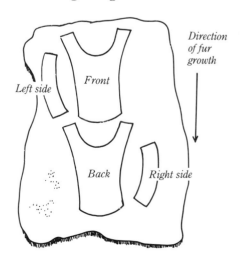

Direction of fur growth

Left side *Front*

Back *Right side*

5. Trace around the patterns with a sharp razor knife, cutting the skin only. Place the fur plastron pieces with the right sides together and stitch the shoulder seams. Place the plastron fur side piece and the side linings with the right sides together and stitch the top seam.

6. Trim the fur away from the ends of each of the plastron side pieces.

Place the fur side pieces over the sides of the base, straddling them. Apply glue to the ends of the left side piece, overlap them over the outer edges of the base and glue them to it. Repeat this step for the right side at the front of the base only. Stitch a snap to the back opening.

Apply the glue to the front of the base (the side which hasn't been lined with silk) and press the skin side of the fur plastron to the base. Work carefully around the whole base, gluing it to the plastron. Keep a large damp rag near your work area to wipe your hands frequently. When the glue is dry, turn under the raw edges of the side lining and stitch it to the skirt.

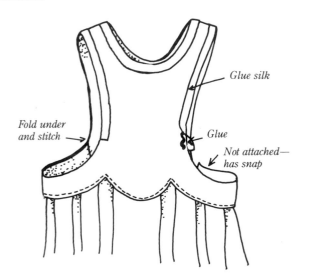

Glue silk

Fold under
and stitch

Glue

Not attached—
has snap

Hem the dress by stitching seam binding to the lower edge and blind stitch the binding to the skirt.

7. Glue the velvet ribbon to the neck edge. Sew 4-6 buttons down the center front of the plastron.

8. To dress the doll, slip the cotehardie over the doll's head and pass the right arm through the opening first.

Horned Headdress

1. Trace the patterns onto the buckram and cut them out. Bend the tabs down and apply glue to each tab. Fit the front to the mid-section and hold them until the glue is secure. Glue the back section. When it is dry, use your fingers to push the angular edges down to give the horns a rounded shape.

2. Glue the horns to the center piece to join them together.

3. Make covers for the horns from a neutral color of smooth knit fabric. Mark the seams, pin them together and sew them by hand, matching the seams, and secure the knit to the horns with a small amount of tacky glue. When the glue is dry, spray the horns with gold paint.

4. Glue a small piece of black velvet ribbon to cover the center piece.

5. Stretch the wired gold mesh ribbon edges around to the front seam and attach them with gold thread. Use tweezers to pull the needle through the stiff fabric.

6. If wired ribbon is not available, fishnet stockings or heavyweight hair nets may be substituted, but they must be attached before the spray paint is applied.

7. Glue the velvet ribbon around the edges carefully.

8. Cut a small piece of mesh ribbon to fit inside the back opening and glue it in place.

Padded Roll

1. Cut the roll pattern pieces on the bias, place the pieces with the right sides together and stitch the roll. Turn the roll right side out using a small safety pin as a turning tool. Stuff the roll carefully (see E4), but don't fill it too tightly. Shape it a bit flat and use very little stuffing at the ends.

2. Stitch on a row of gold beads and glue a glass jewel in the front center. (See Step 4 below for making the setting for the glass jewel.) Pin the roll around the horned headdress, with the ends of the roll at the back of the headdress. Tack the roll to the horns in several places and sew the ends of the roll together, turning the raw ends inside.

3. To secure the headdress to the doll's head, use three black-headed pins placed in the black velvet ribbon.

4. Make two settings for the glass jewel—one for the headdress and one for the crown. Roll out a thin sheet of plasticine clay (Sculpey® or Fimo). Press the gem into the clay and cut the excess clay away.

Make eight tiny clay balls and press one at each side of the jewel base for the jewel. Remove the jewel and bake the clay in the oven according to package directions. When the clay is cool, paint the base and glue the glass jewel in place.

Crown

1. Trace the crown pattern onto stiff art paper or bristol board. (Sheet styrene, .01" thick, available at hobby shops, is sturdier.) Use small sharp scissors to cut out the crown.

Glue a reinforcing strip of the same paper to the back side of the crown.

2. Cut 5 mm. wooden beads in half with a razor knife and glue them to each side of the crown's knobs.

3. Spray the crown with gold paint. Glue the white stones in the center of the finials and position the clay-base jewel onto the front center finial.

4. Carefully shape the crown onto the headdress. Fit it flat against the back side of the padded roll. Glue the connecting strip to join the ends with the tab bent upward. The tab slips under the net to hold the crown in place. Glue the crown to the headdress in several places to secure it.

Shoes

1. Place the pattern on the wrong side of red or gold leather. Trace around the pattern and cut out the shoes. Place the shoes with the right sides of leather together and machine stitch using a small needle and taking small stitches.

2. Glue the seam flat except at the toe.

3. Make a window from white glove leather. Place gold cord in a lattice shape and use the gold embroidery thread to couch it in place (see C8). Glue the window into the opening, with the upper edge of the window even with the sides of the shoes.

4. Start at the outside of the shoe and glue the strap around the upper back, inside and window, overlapping the strap on the outside. Slip the shoe onto the doll's foot.

Final details

Add a short chain (a small bracelet would be the right size) to hang around the doll's neck and a link from a gold chain will be the right size to put on her right index finger. When you display the doll, the skirt and train on the surcote are not full; instead, they should hang straight down and puddle around her feet.

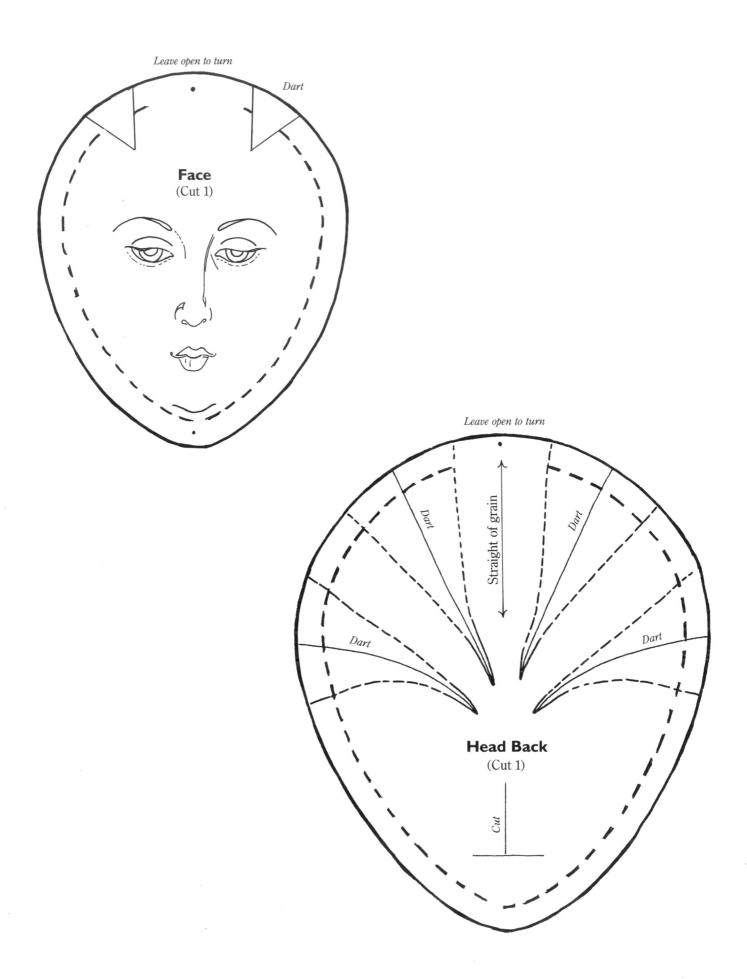

Leave open to turn

Dart

Face
(Cut 1)

Leave open to turn

Dart

Straight of grain

Dart

Dart

Dart

Dart

Head Back
(Cut 1)

Cut

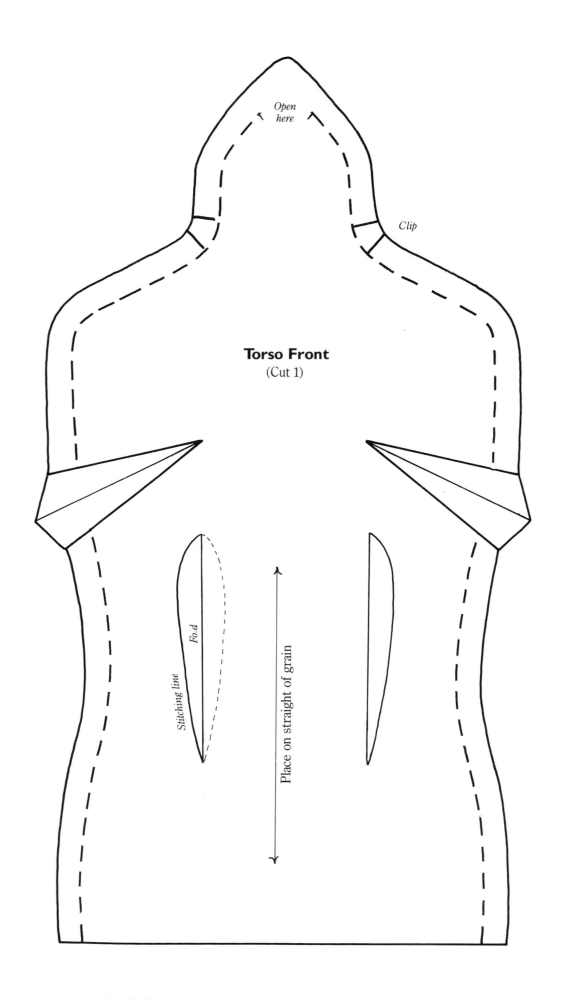

Open
here

Clip

Torso Front
(Cut 1)

Stitching line

Fold

Place on straight of grain

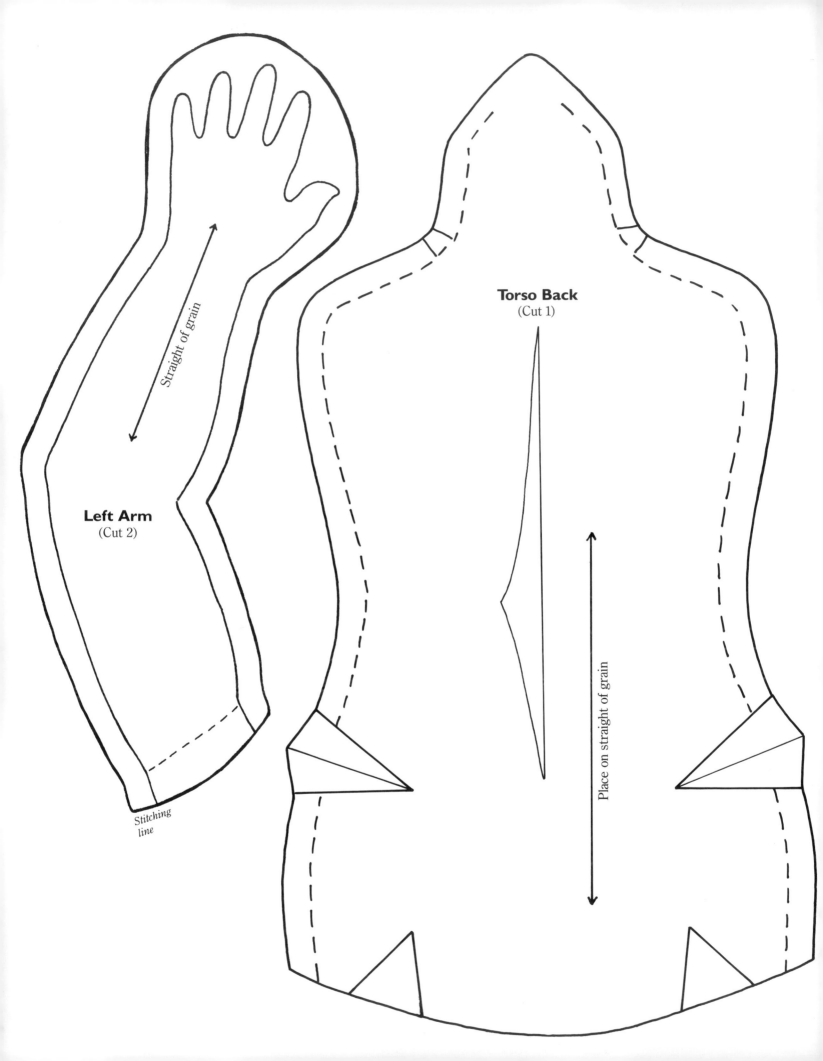

Straight of grain

Left Arm
(Cut 2)

Stitching
line

Torso Back
(Cut 1)

Place on straight of grain

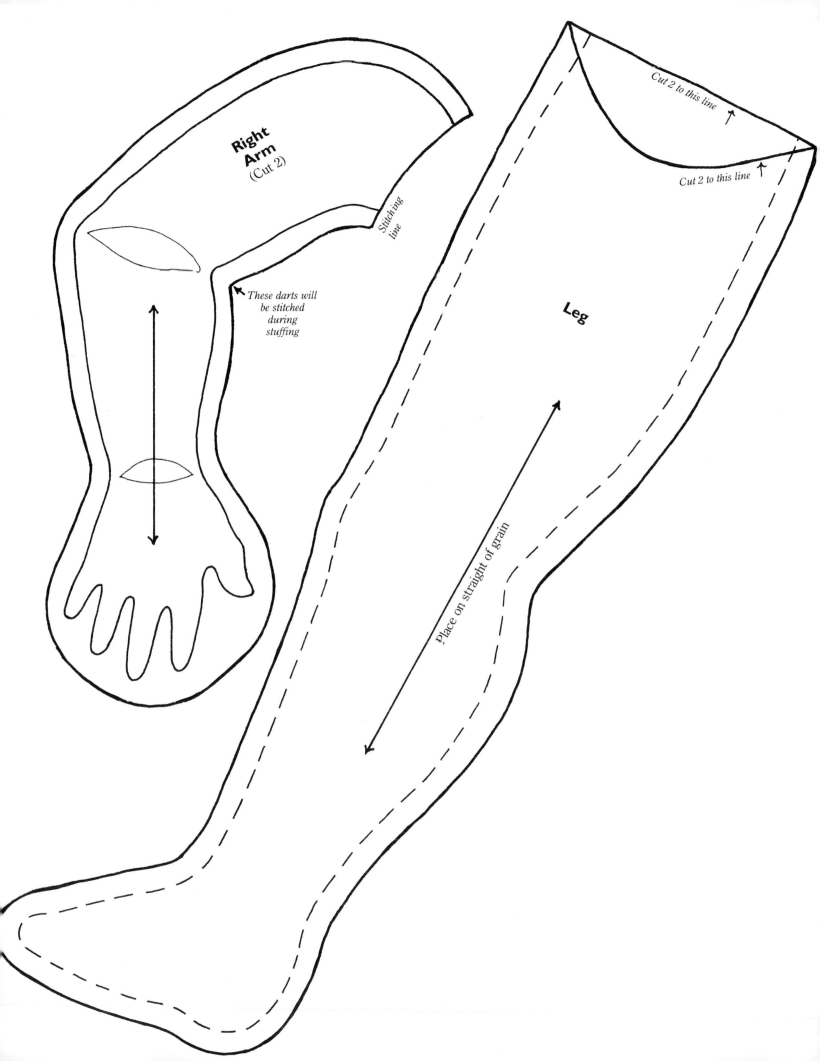

Right Arm
(Cut 2)

Stitching line

These darts will be stitched during stuffing

Leg

Place on straight of grain

Cut 2 to this line

Cut 2 to this line

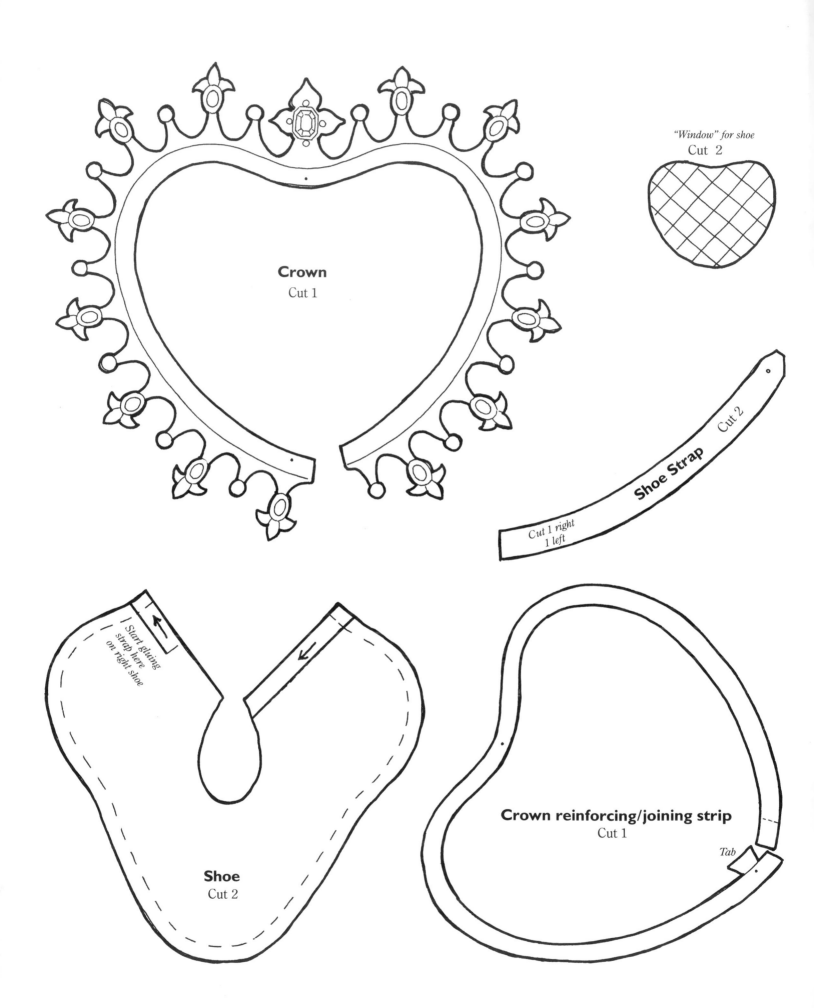

Crown
Cut 1

"Window" for shoe
Cut 2

Shoe Strap
Cut 2

Cut 1 right
1 left

Start gluing strap here on right shoe

Shoe
Cut 2

Crown reinforcing/joining strip
Cut 1

Tab

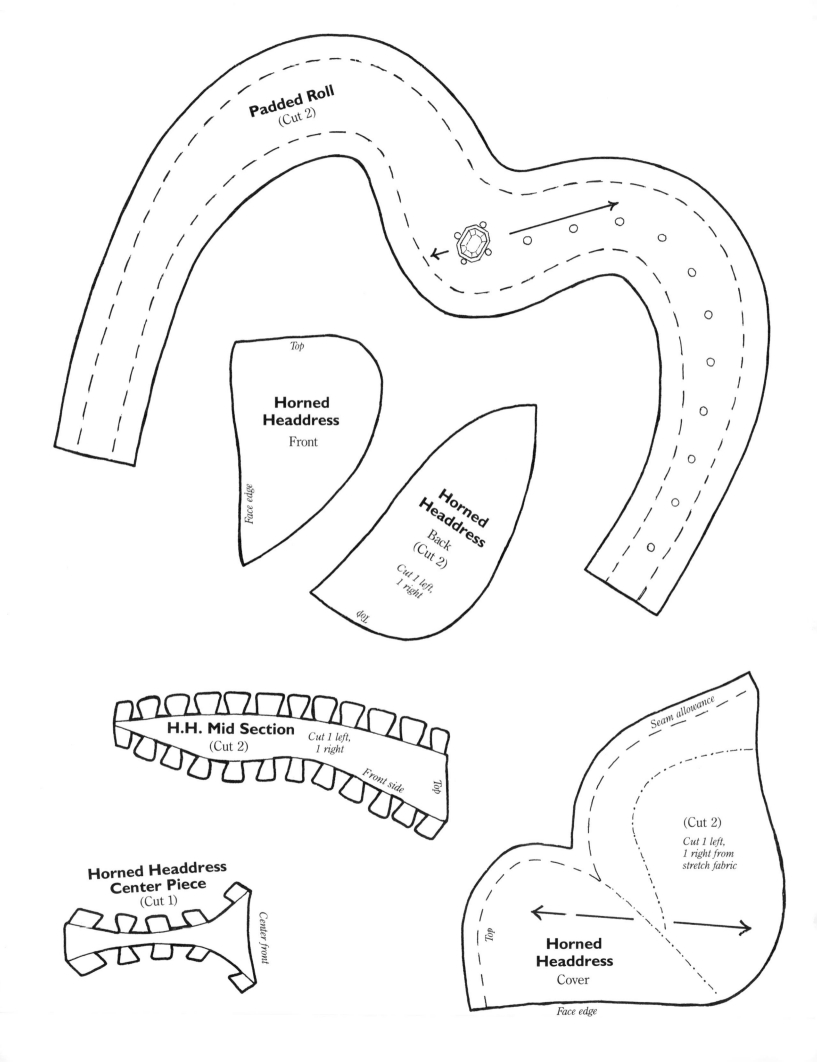

Padded Roll
(Cut 2)

Horned Headdress
Front

Top

Face edge

Horned Headdress
Back
(Cut 2)

Cut 1 left,
1 right

Top

H.H. Mid Section
(Cut 2)

Cut 1 left,
1 right

Front side

Top

Horned Headdress Center Piece
(Cut 1)

Center front

Seam allowance

(Cut 2)

Cut 1 left,
1 right from
stretch fabric

Top

Horned Headdress
Cover

Face edge

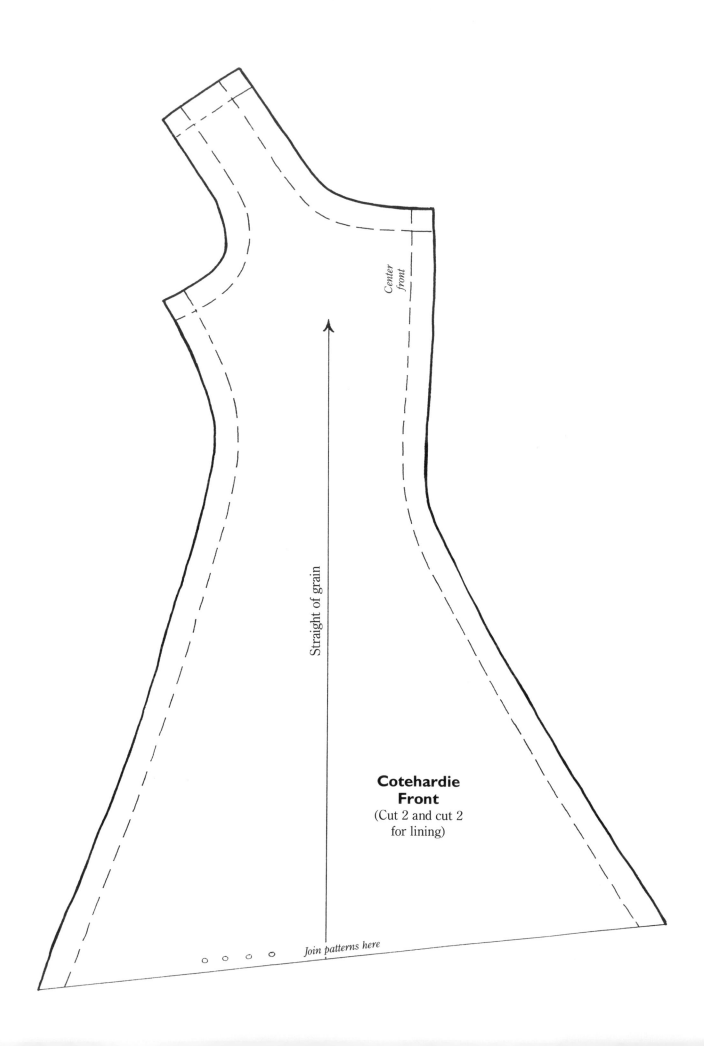

Straight of grain

Center front

Cotehardie Front
(Cut 2 and cut 2 for lining)

Join patterns here

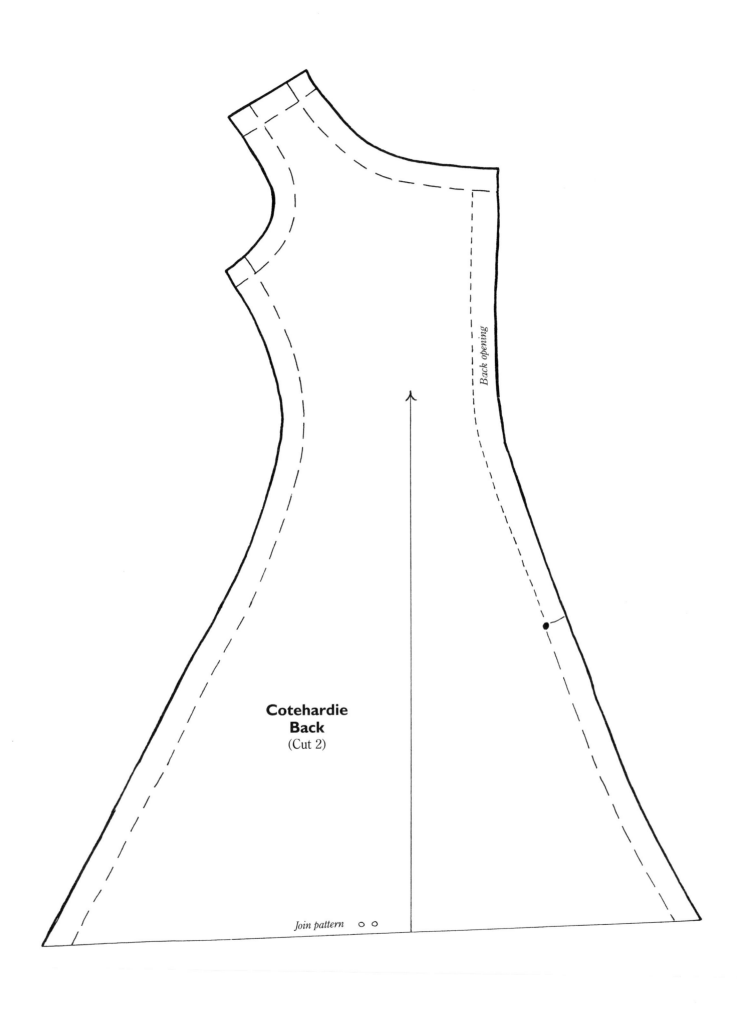

**Cotehardie
Back**
(Cut 2)

Back opening

Join pattern ○ ○

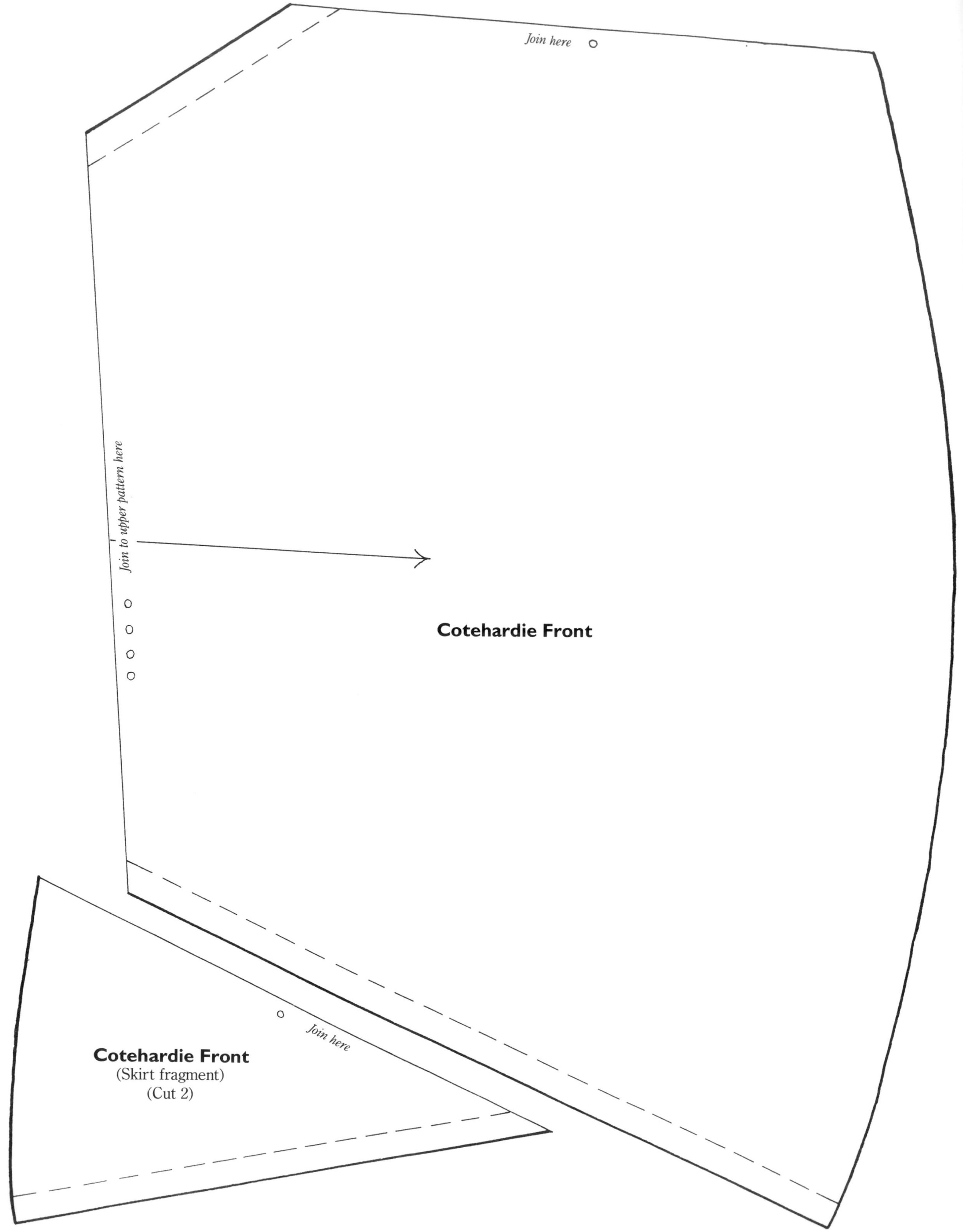

Join here o

Join to upper pattern here

o
o
o
o
o

Cotehardie Front

Cotehardie Front
(Skirt fragment)
(Cut 2)

o *Join here*

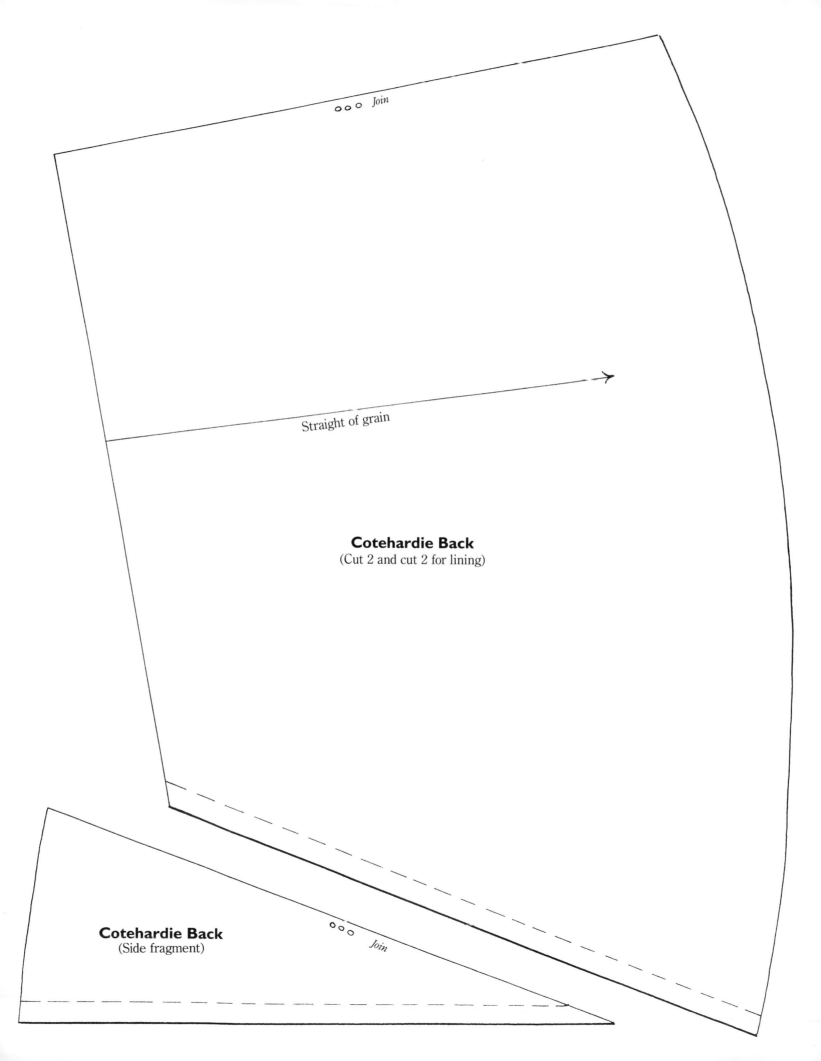

Join

Straight of grain

Cotehardie Back
(Cut 2 and cut 2 for lining)

Cotehardie Back
(Side fragment)

Join

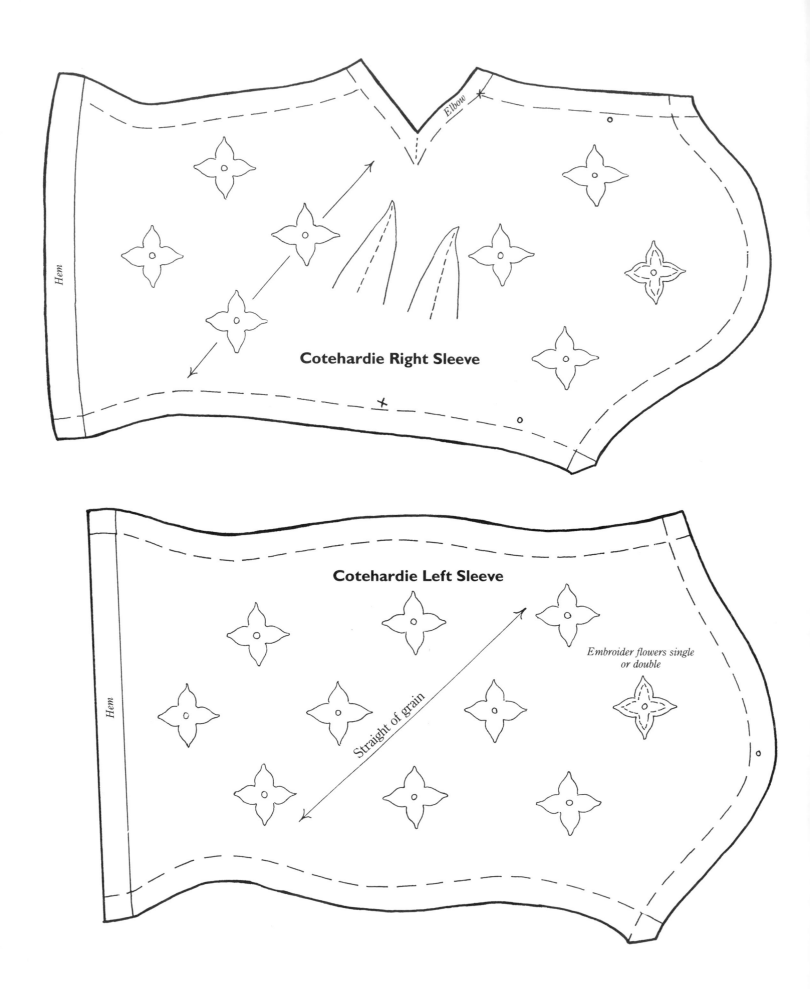

Cotehardie Right Sleeve

Elbow

Hem

Cotehardie Left Sleeve

Hem

Straight of grain

*Embroider flowers single
or double*

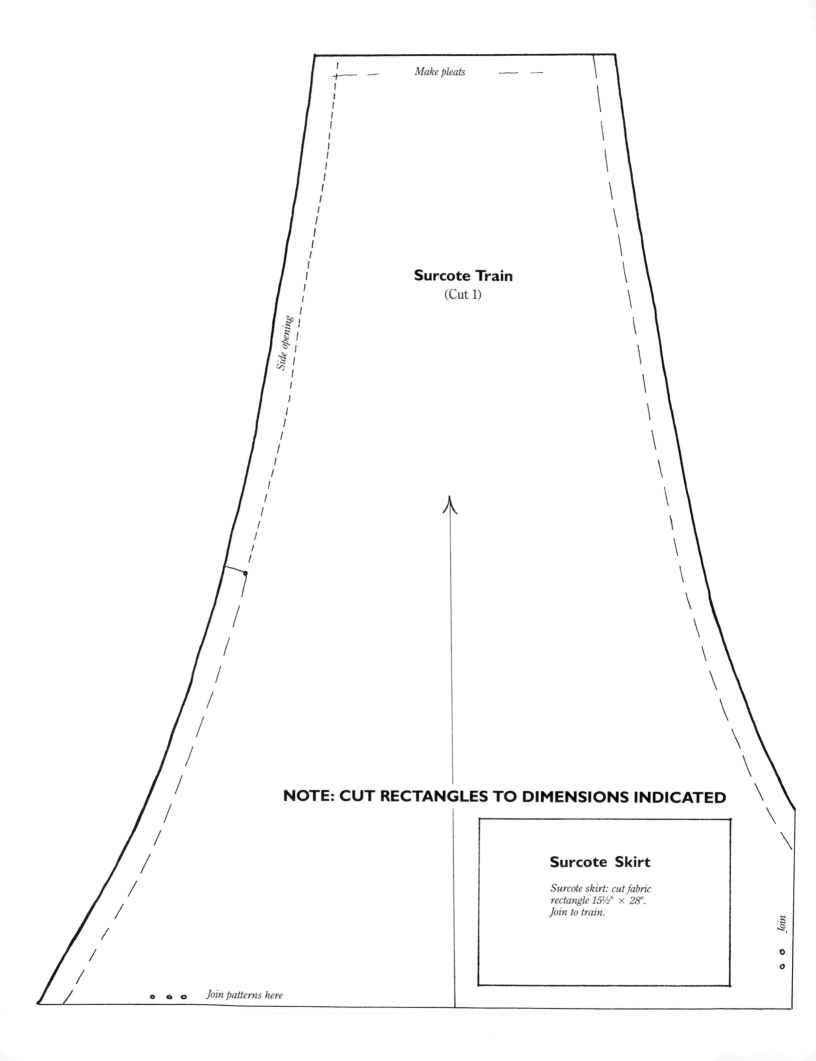

Make pleats

Surcote Train
(Cut 1)

Side opening

NOTE: CUT RECTANGLES TO DIMENSIONS INDICATED

Surcote Skirt

Surcote skirt: cut fabric rectangle 15½" × 28". Join to train.

Join

Join patterns here

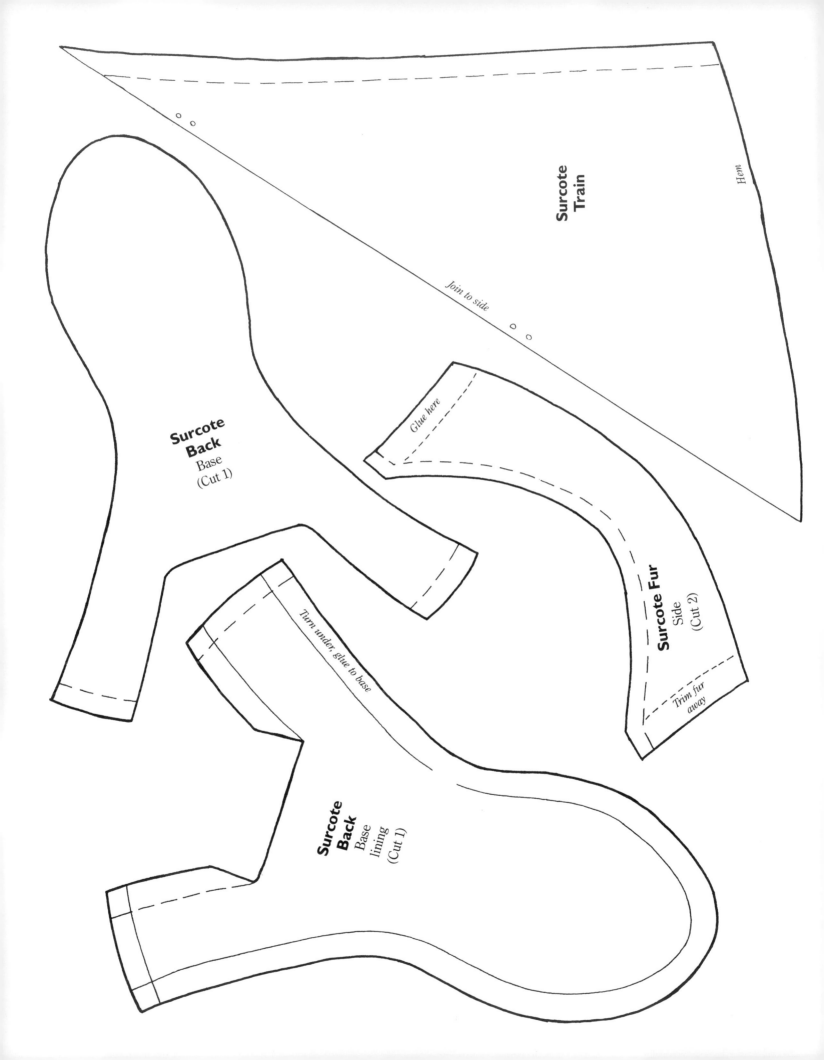

Surcote Train

Hem

Join to side

Surcote Back
Base
(Cut 1)

Glue here

Surcote Fur
Side
(Cut 2)

Trim fur away

Turn under, glue to base

Surcote Back
Base lining
(Cut 1)

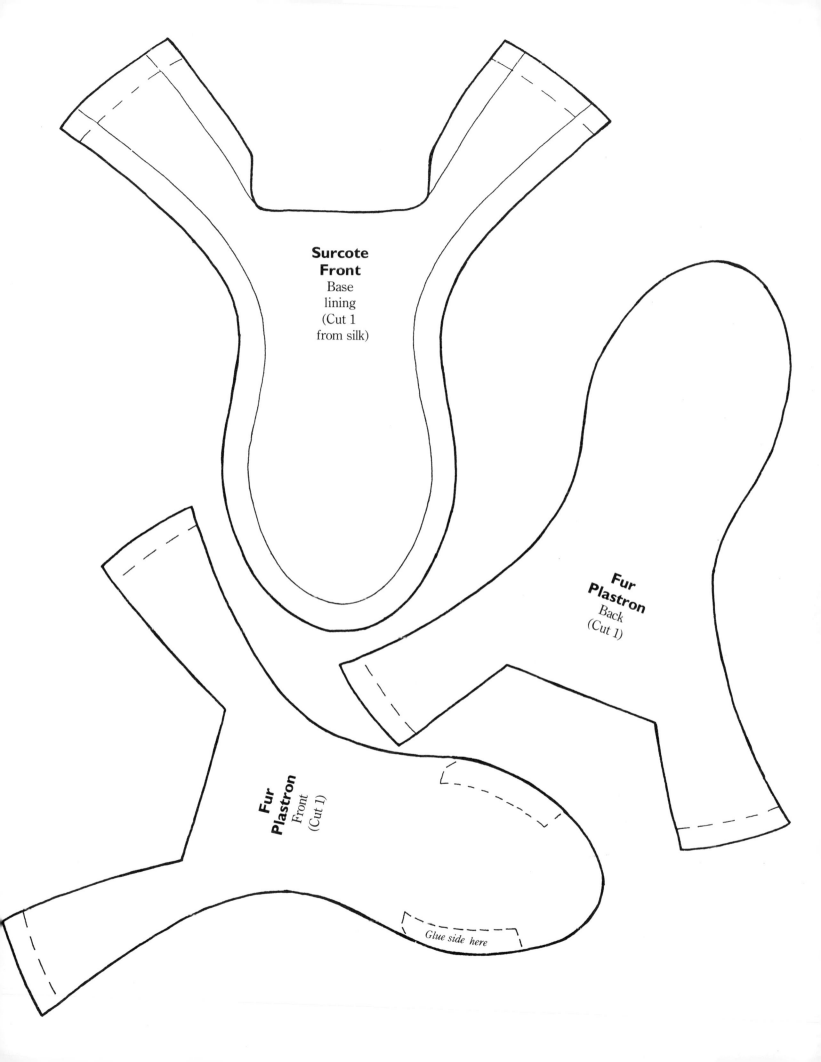

Surcote Front
Base
lining
(Cut 1
from silk)

Fur Plastron
Back
(Cut 1)

Fur Plastron
Front
(Cut 1)

Glue side here

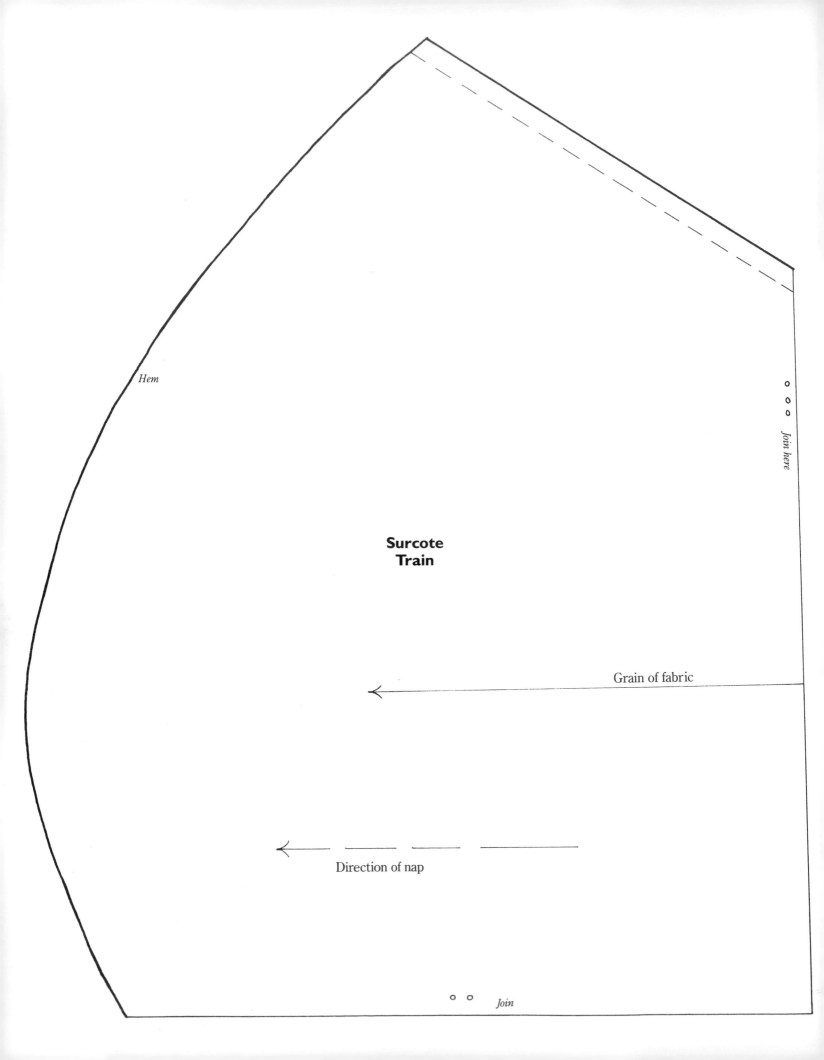

Hem

**Surcote
Train**

Join here

Grain of fabric

← - - - - - - - - -

Direction of nap

∘ ∘ *Join*

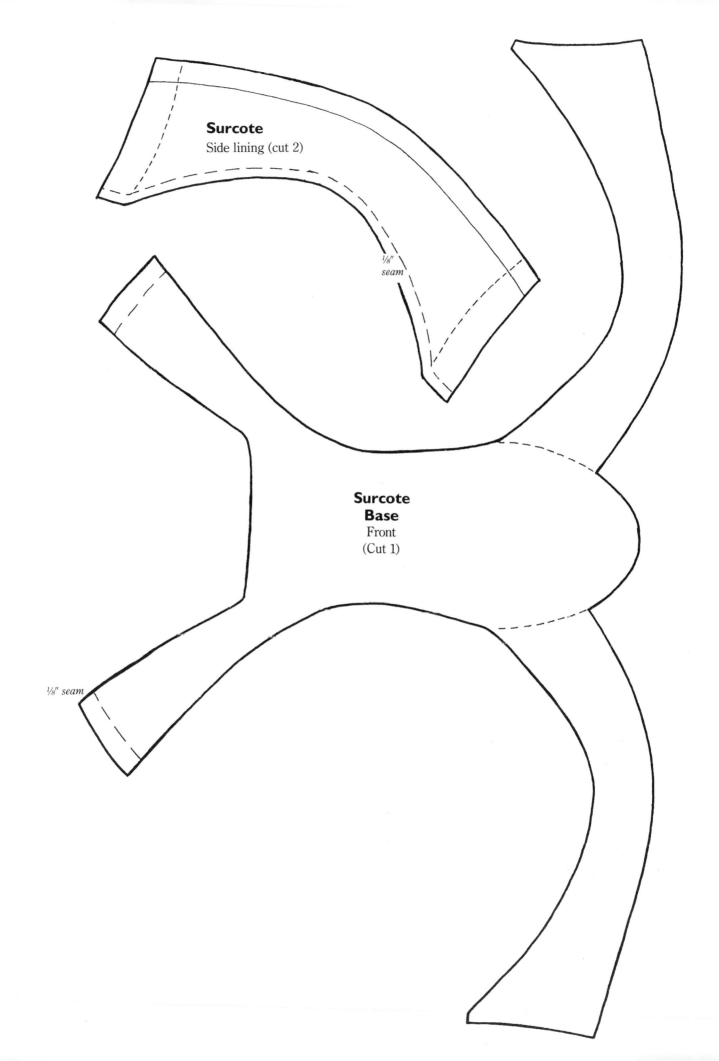

Surcote
Side lining (cut 2)

*⅛"
seam*

**Surcote
Base**
Front
(Cut 1)

⅛" seam

Old-fashioned
MARY RUTH

by Roxanne Becker

I met Roxanne at Quilt Market, when I stopped to look at the wonderful soft-sculpture patterns which she and her sister publish. Roxanne lives in Carrollton, Texas, and her sister lives in Minnesota, but they seem to have a marvelous long-distance relationship. Roxanne has an ability to create simple, well-constructed decorative patterns for her business, yet she is able to create one-of-a-kind pieces that are involved and intricate. She recently created a beautiful doll depicting a Viking woman awaiting the return of her husband. The doll was dressed in a carefully researched, authentically constructed Viking costume; her beautiful red hair was of hand-dyed hemp. I liked the idea so well, I asked her to construct an old-fashioned doll using the hemp.

This doll is named Mary Ruth, after Roxanne's maternal grandmother. Roxanne used the kind of soft colors which reminded her of this grandmother. She says: "I believe in Michaelangelo's theory of sculpting to let the figure in the stone reveal itself. In my case, I try to let the doll emerge from a pile of fabrics, trims, etc. As things start to 'click,' I can feel a 'personality' emerging. It's my job to decide just 'who' it is.

"Antique and primitive-type dolls hold a fascination for me. It was my intent to try to replicate a doll that could possibly have been made when my grandmother was a girl. Muslin, calico, bits of eyelet or lace saved from an old piece of clothing, an odd button or two, real hair, corn silk, yarn or string (or even rope) might have been used to make a doll.

"Mary Ruth is a memory-making kind of doll employing, if possible, used fabrics and odds and ends, even if they don't all match. Tan or tea-dyeing gives that impression of age and use that softens the whole effect.

"Mary Ruth, like my grandmother, or any girl around the turn of the century, has a limited wardrobe: one pair of high-top buttoned shoes, two pairs of pantaloons (one a little fancier than the other, trimmed with ribbons), two eyelet-trimmed petticoats (one short, one long), a long-sleeved calico 'everyday' dress, a pinafore to protect her dress when she does her daily chores, a special calico dress and a flat-crowned straw hat with ribbons to protect her from getting too much sun when working outdoors."

This is the kind of doll that should incorporate your family treasures. If you have a piece of fabric from an old dress which belonged to someone dear to you, or if you have fabric that reminds you of someone special, use it. Create an heirloom to pass on to your own family.

MATERIALS LIST

(100% cottons used throughout)

2/3 yard of unbleached muslin for body, arms, and legs, petticoat and pantaloons

1 bag stuffing fiber

2 yards of 1/2″-diameter 3-ply natural hemp rope for hair (You may substitute 1 skein baby or sport yarn, heavy crochet thread, or wool roving.)

Best Dress

1/2 yard of calico

1 yard of 1″-wide flat ivory lace

1/3 yard of narrow picot trim

1 yard of 1″-wide double-faced satin ribbon for sash

Everyday Dress

1/3 yard of calico

Embroidery floss for drawstrings (Anchor 0392 may be used)

Rit® dye (tan, tangerine, golden yellow, and cocoa brown)

Fabric paints (light brown, light peach or pink)

Powdered blush

Cotton swabs

Black permanent-ink fine-tip marking pen

Round wood toothpicks

Hot glue gun and glue sticks

1/4″-wide old-looking button for back of pinafore

Matching thread

4″-wide flat-crowned straw hat

1 yard of 1/4″-wide satin ribbon (for hat)

Note: Mary Ruth's party dress has a lace-trimmed, gathered bodice and drop shoulder with full three-quarter-length sleeves. Three rows of gathering pulls in her empire waistline, and the dress is embellished with a 1″-wide double-sided satin ribbon sash tied into a bow in the back. The bottom of her skirt has a 1/4″-deep tuck trimming the hemline. Mary Ruth can wear her fancy knee-length or her ankle-length pantaloons and petticoat, depending on whether she wants her eyelet trim to show or not.

Mary Ruth's everyday dress has a high-necked bodice, drop-shoulder long sleeves which are gathered at the wrist with embroidery floss drawstrings, and a plain gathered skirt that comes to the top of her boots.

CONSTRUCTION

Doll Body

1. Cut the doll body, arms and legs from unbleached muslin, following directions at B2, B3 and B4. Lightly trace the facial features and the boot line with a pencil. The fabric can be dyed tan with Rit® Dye or tea-dyed before cutting out the body or after sewing it, according to directions at A2.

2. After you sew the darts on the lower back of the torso, trim the seam to 1/8″ and sew the body front and back together, leaving an opening where indicated (see E3).

3. Stuff the lower legs firmly to within 1″ of the knee line.

4. Point the toe of the shoe forward and match the leg seams. Poke the fabric in on the sides of the knee to form tucks, stitch across the knee line and stuff the upper leg to within 1″ of the top of the leg. Refer to E4, E6, and E9. Pleat the open end of the leg as you did for the knee and stitch it across to close it.

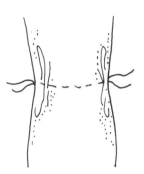

5. Stuff the hands as directed at E5 (Step A). Stuff the arm to within 1″ of the elbow and stitch the elbow with the top seam directly over the bottom seam (the thumb will be sticking up toward you).

6. Stuff the upper arm to within 1″ of the open end, poke the sides in to form a pleat and sew across the top end.

7. Insert the arms and legs into the doll's body as indicated in E14.

Painting the Face and the Boots

1. Spray the face and feet with fast-drying matte acrylic sealer and allow it to dry.

2. Make any necessary adjustments on the facial features with a pencil.

3. Squeeze a drop or two of brown fabric paint on a mixing palette. Add a couple of drops of water to dilute the paint. Test it on a scrap of fabric to determine the desired concentration or darkness, as the same colors will look different on tea-dyed fabric and unbleached muslin.

4. Dip the tip of a toothpick into the fabric dye and paint the eye above the crease and down the sides of the nose and under the nose to form shadows. Lightly outline the lips.

5. Two or three applications can give an adequate amount of color to the eyelids and the eyebrows.

6. Add a bit more dye if you want the eyes to be dark brown, and paint the iris color.

7. Use a soft peachy-pink for a natural lip color.

8. Allow the paint to dry thoroughly.

9. Use a black fine-tip permanent-ink marking pen to outline the eyes and eyelashes, the nostrils, the crease in the lips and the pupils in the eyes.

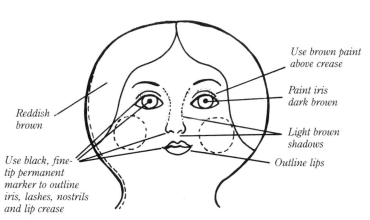

Reddish brown

Use brown paint above crease

Paint iris dark brown

Light brown shadows

Outline lips

Use black, fine-tip permanent marker to outline iris, lashes, nostrils and lip crease

10. Use a soft brush to apply pink powder blush to the cheek area.

11. Mix a larger amount of brown fabric dye and water for the boots and paint them, starting at the penciled line at the top. The spray sealer will prevent the wash from running beyond the penciled edge. Allow the paint to dry thoroughly. Use the black fine-tip permanent-ink marking pen to draw the boot flaps and buttons.

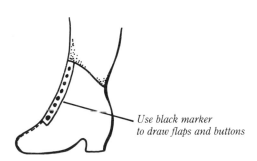

Use black marker to draw flaps and buttons

Doll Hair

1. Separate the plies of the hemp rope and cut them into 15″ lengths. Unravel the plies to separate the individual strands.

2. Dye Mary Ruth's hair according to the instructions at F4.

3. Place the dyed hemp strands side by side on a 6″ square of fabric. Follow the instructions at F6, Step 5 and 8-9. Use thread which matches the hair fiber.

4. Trim the fabric 1/8″ from the stitching. The fabric strip will make an ideal place to apply the glue when the wig is attached to the doll's head. A light application of hot glue along the hairline in front and back of the ears will help keep the hair in place.

5. Pull each half of the doll's hair to the side of the head

and tack the strands of hemp to the doll's head just under the area where her ears would be.

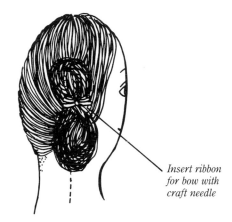

Insert ribbon for bow with craft needle

6. Twist each hank of the hair to form a loop or figure 8. Trim the ends and tack the hair to the doll's head.

7. Thread a large blunt craft needle with 1/4″-wide satin ribbon.

Thread the ribbon through the top part of each side of the hairdo, just above the ear area, and tie it into bows.

CLOTHING

Pantaloons

Follow the instructions at G1 (Steps 1, 3, 4B, 5B or C, 6 and 7).

Petticoat

Follow the instructions at G2 (Steps 1-4).

Pinafore

Follow the instructions at G9 (Steps 1-2, 9-14, 16 and 18).

Everyday Dress

Follow instructions G3 (Steps 1-2A and 3), G1 (Step 5A), G3 (Steps 5-7, 11 and 15A-C).

Party Dress

Follow the instructions at G4 and trim the neck and sleeve openings with lace.

Hat

Make a small opening in the sides of the hat brim, close to the crown, and insert a ribbon up through one hole, around the crown and down through the other hole. Tack the ribbon to the hat to secure it. Tie the ribbon in a loose bow if you want to slip the hat off the doll's head and onto her back.

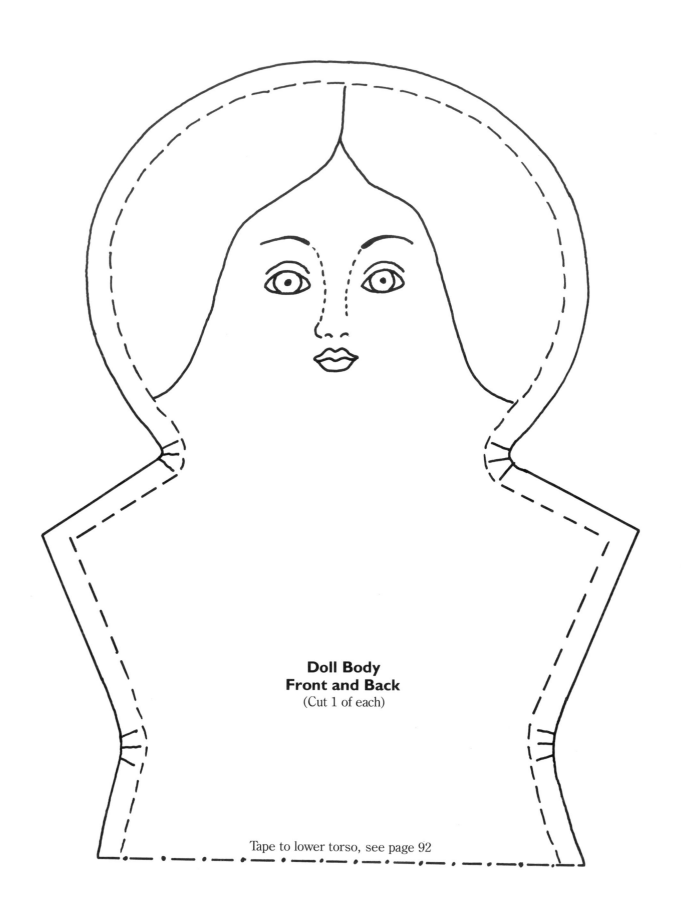

**Doll Body
Front and Back**
(Cut 1 of each)

Tape to lower torso, see page 92

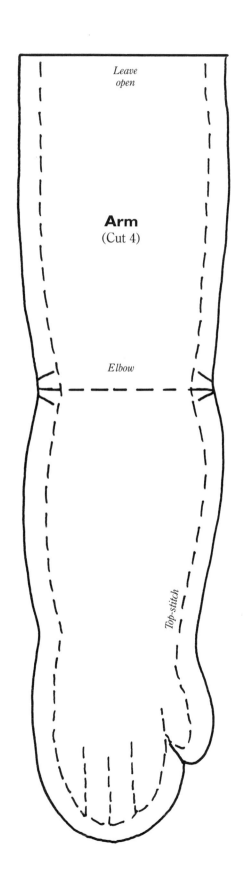

Arm
(Cut 4)

Leave open

Elbow

Top-stitch

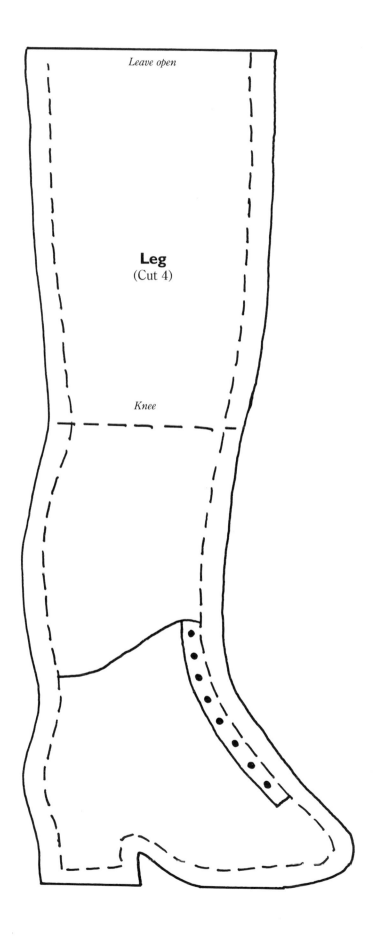

Leg
(Cut 4)

Leave open

Knee

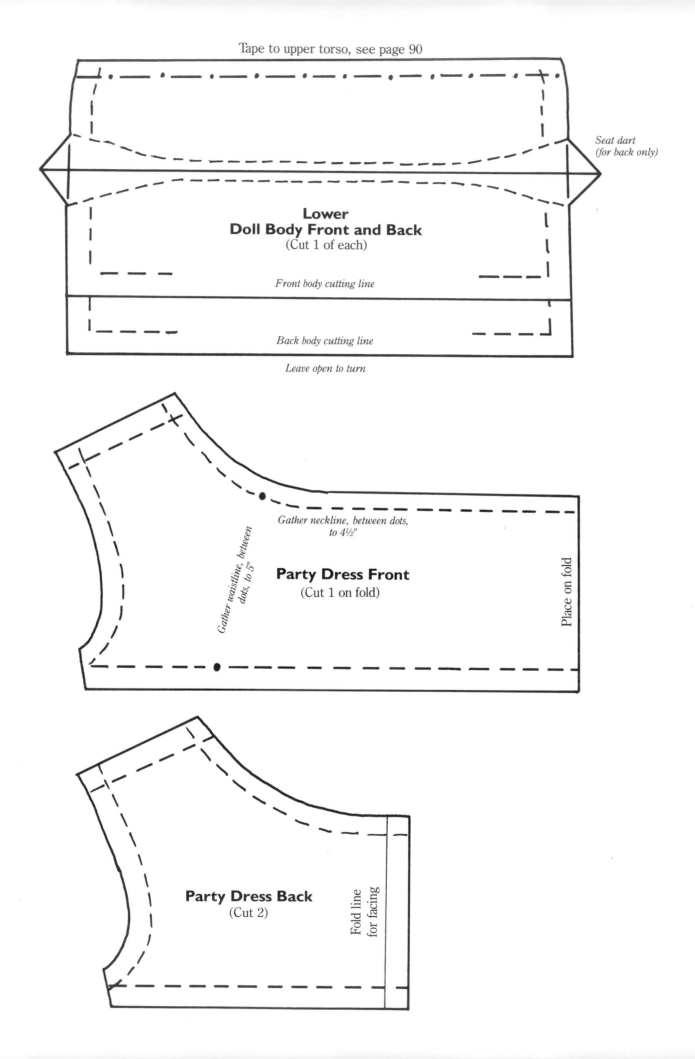

Tape to upper torso, see page 90

Seat dart
(for back only)

**Lower
Doll Body Front and Back**
(Cut 1 of each)

Front body cutting line

Back body cutting line

Leave open to turn

Gather neckline, between dots,
to 4½″

Gather waistline, between
dots, to 5″

Party Dress Front
(Cut 1 on fold)

Place on fold

Party Dress Back
(Cut 2)

Fold line
for facing

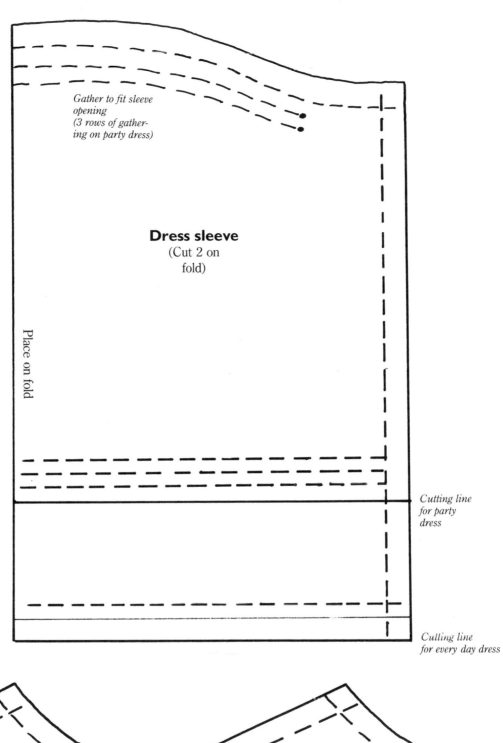

Gather to fit sleeve opening (3 rows of gathering on party dress)

Dress sleeve
(Cut 2 on fold)

Place on fold

Cutting line for party dress

Culling line for every day dress

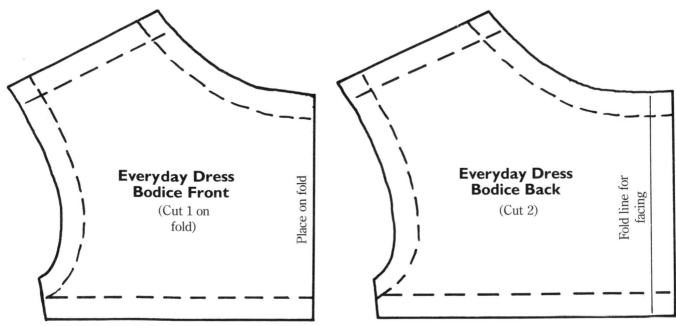

Everyday Dress Bodice Front
(Cut 1 on fold)

Place on fold

Everyday Dress Bodice Back
(Cut 2)

Fold line for facing

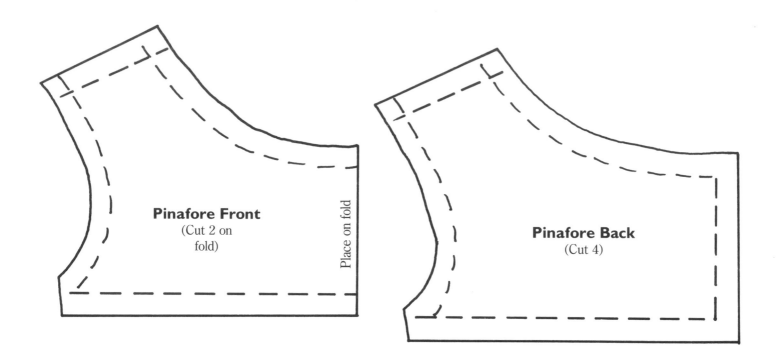

Pinafore Front
(Cut 2 on fold)

Place on fold

Pinafore Back
(Cut 4)

Pinafore Pocket
(Cut 1)

Cut a 3" square for the handker-chief. Pink the edges.

Total length for shorter version (add eyelet lace) is 7⅞"

Total length for longer version is 10⅛"

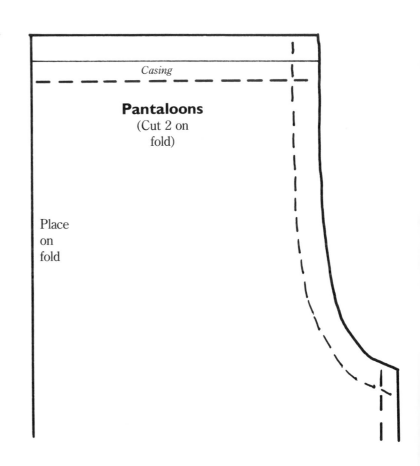

Casing

Pantaloons
(Cut 2 on fold)

Place on fold

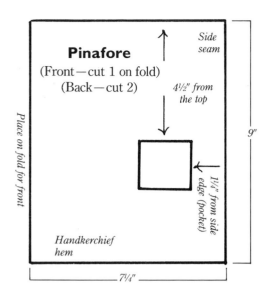

Pinafore

(Front—cut 1 on fold)
(Back—cut 2)

Side seam

4½" from the top

1¼" from side edge (pocket)

Place on fold for front

Handkerchief hem

9"

7¼"

NOTE: CUT RECTANGLES TO DIMENSIONS INDICATED

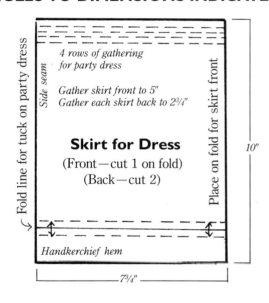

4 rows of gathering for party dress

Gather skirt front to 5"
Gather each skirt back to 2¾"

Skirt for Dress

(Front—cut 1 on fold)
(Back—cut 2)

Side seam

Fold line for tuck on party dress

Place on fold for skirt front

Handkerchief hem

10"

7¾"

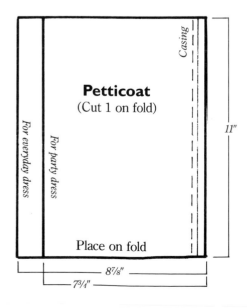

Petticoat

(Cut 1 on fold)

Casing

For everyday dress

For party dress

Place on fold

11"

8⅞"

7¾"

Little Girl
FELICITY AND LUCY

by Cindy Extance

Cindy's background includes a lot of quilting. Her dollmaking is a more recent endeavor. I was impressed by her craftsmanship, since many of her creations are very small. Her dolls are good examples of how important it is to trim loose threads, stuff the doll with care and choose the right hair fiber and fabric.

When my daughter first saw Cindy's dolls a few years ago, she asked if she could buy them. They were just right for a little girl to play with and the wardrobe, which could store so many little belongings, was icing on the cake. When I was thinking of this Little Girl category, one name came into my mind—Cindy.

Cindy wrote: "Felicity was created from dreams I had when I was a girl. I always loved to dress dolls and have a place to keep them, all of their own. I didn't want Felicity to get lonely, so she has her best friend, Lucy, that she can dress, too. She has a Victorian air, because then, as now, dolls were a cherished item."

A few years ago, Cindy moved to North Carolina from Connecticut. She has participated in numerous quilt and dollmaking projects in both states. Her designs have won several awards and have been sold in this country, and as far away as New Zealand.

ringbone stitch and the feather stitch. In addition, the quilt is embellished with beads and charms. Place the 2″ border and quilt with the right sides together and stitch along the edges. Stop the stitching 1/4″ from each corner. Stitch the top borders to the quilt top and miter the corners. Press the seam allowance toward the outside of the quilt.

4. Layer the quilt top, batting and the backing (with the top and backing facing outward). Pin the ribbon-weave lace over the seam between the patchwork and the borders, then stitch it to the quilt. Use a longer stitch length so you don't pucker the backing.

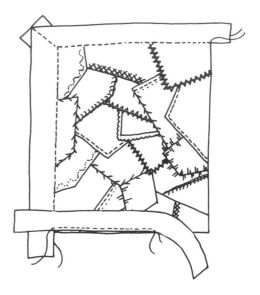

Quilt

1. Cut a 10″×8″ piece of muslin. Cut two 2-1/2″×14″ strips and two 1-1/2″×12″ strips for the borders. Cut 1-1/2 yards of 2″ wide bias to bind the edges (the binding fabric is the same as the border fabric). You will also need a 12″×10″ piece of thin cotton batting or flannel.

2. Start in the center of the muslin and build a crazy-patch design. Many of the pieces in Cindy's quilt are triangular, but you can use any shape you like. Fold under 1/4″ of the edges and overlap the previous shape by stitching the pieces to each other by hand.

5. Fold the bias strip in half and press it. Open it back up and place it on the right side of the quilt, with the right sides together and matching the raw edges. Stitch 1/4″ from the edge of the quilt. Stop 1/4″ from each corner and miter the corners. Fold the bias over the raw edges and fold under 1/4″ of the raw edge of the bias strip. Stitch it to the back side of the quilt. Weave 1/2″ ribbon through the lace and tie a bow at each corner.

Felicity's Wardrobe

1. Use a razor knife to cut the following pieces from the art board: One 10″×15″ piece for the back, two 5″×15″ pieces for the sides, two 5″×10-1/4″ pieces for the top and bottom, two 5″×15-1/4″ pieces for the doors and two 1″×1/2″ pieces for the dowel supports. Use the pattern to cut the curved tops of the doors. From the oak tag cut one 9-3/4″×14-3/4″ piece for the back, two 4-3/4″×14-3/4″ pieces for the sides, two 4-3/4″×10″ pieces for the top and bottom and two 4-3/4″×15″ pieces for the doors. Cut the curve at the tops of the doors as you did previously.

2. Lay the larger pieces on the wrong side of the fabric you have chosen for the outside of the wardrobe. Leave a 1″ border around the pieces of art board. Pick each piece up

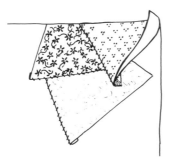

3. Add the trims and lace in the seams as you stitch the pieces together. Trim the patchwork to the edge of the muslin when you are finished and add any embroidery you desire. Cindy has used several of the stitches at C8. Among these are the French knot, which is used to tack the ribbon to one of the odd-shaped pieces, the straight stitch and lazy daisy stitch (used to make an embroidered fan), a her-

and apply a light coat of glue with a sponge brush. Press the art board onto the fabric firmly and run your hand over the board to remove any air bubbles. –OR– You may use a fusible web to bond the art board to the fabric. Apply the web to the wrong side of the fabric, following the directions on the package, and trace the outlines of each piece of art board onto the paper side of the webbing. Leave a 1″ border around each piece of board. This extra fabric will enable you to wrap the fabric around the edges of the board so they don't show.

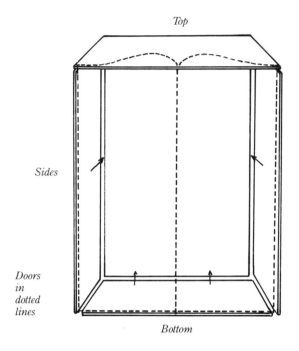

3. Clip the fabric across the corners of each piece of board. If you have chosen to glue the fabric onto the board, apply glue to the edges of the fabric, fold it over the edges of the board to the wrong side and allow the glue to dry. If you are applying the fabric with the fusible web, remove the paper and fuse the fabric around the edges.

4. Cover the oak tag pieces with the lining fabric, following the same procedures as above.

5. Make the pockets from the lining fabric. Cut two 10″ × 5″ pieces and one 10″ × 10″ piece. Zig zag the raw edges of each piece. Press under 3/8″ on one 10″ side for each of the pieces, then press under 1/4″ on all the remaining sides. Stitch close to the zig zagged edge on the 3/8″ edges. This will form the casing for the elastic. Cut three 6″ lengths of elastic and feed them through the casings. Top-stitch only the sides of each piece, close to the folded edge, stitching through the elastic to hold it in place.

6. Crease the center of each pocket at the bottom edge, make a 3/4″ box pleat and baste it.

7. You will be attaching the pockets to the door pieces with the lining fabric on them. Wrap 1″ of the sides and the bottom edge of the pocket around to the back side of the

right-side door. Glue all three sides of the pocket onto the back side of the oak tag door linings.

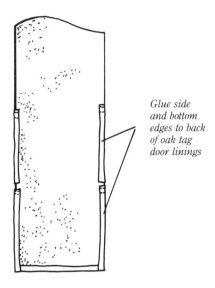

Glue side and bottom edges to back of oak tag door linings

Repeat this procedure for the left door, where you will attach two pockets. One of the smaller pockets will be attached to the door about halfway down. Pin the sides of the pocket so they wrap around the back of the door lining. The lower edge of the pocket will be folded under 1/4″ and glued.

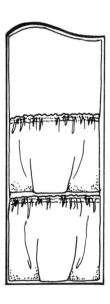

8. On each front door (covered art board), measure up 6″ from the bottom and 1/4″ from the center edge and mark it with a pencil. Use a sturdy needle to sew the button on each door where you have marked it. Use double quilting thread and go back and forth three times before you make a knot and cut the thread. Glue the grosgrain ribbon to the front edges of the side pieces.

9. Hot glue all the lining pieces to the covered art board pieces (except for the doors), leaving a 1/8″ border all around.

10. Glue the side piece to the top piece, butting the lining together.

Repeat for the other side and the bottom edge.

11. Glue the back onto the wardrobe.

12. Lay the wardrobe on its side and place the door (covered art board) next to it, lining up the bottom and side edges. Glue the other half of the grosgrain ribbon to the wrong side of the door.

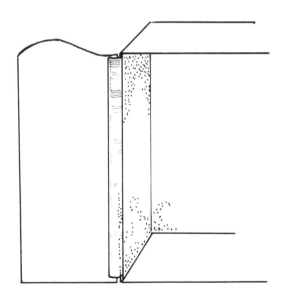

13. Hot glue the lining to the door, leaving a 1/8″ border all around.

14. Paint the dowel with two or three coats of a co-ordinating color.

15. Place the dowel at the top of the 1″ x 1-1/2″ boards and draw a half-circle.

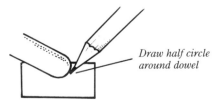

Draw half circle around dowel

16. Cover a 1″ × 3″ piece of oak tag with the lining fabric. Make a fold 7/8″ from the top and hot glue one of the pieces with the half circle to the bottom of the covered oak tag.

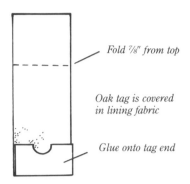

Fold ⅞″ from top

Oak tag is covered in lining fabric

Glue onto tag end

Hot glue the end of the dowel into the half circle of each piece of art board. Glue the folded end of the covered oak tag about halfway back in the wardrobe, with the other end of the dowel on the inside wall of the wardrobe, as shown.

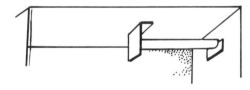

17. To decorate the outside of the doors, lightly pencil 1/2″ from the sides of the doors, except at the center where the button is. Mark two horizontal lines 1/4″ from the center of the button. Measure 1-7/8″ from the outside edges and make two 1-7/8″ × 5-1/4″ rectangles in the bottom half of the door.

Apply a small bead of tacky glue with a toothpick along the inside of each line and press on 1/8″ ribbon. Cut the pieces to fit, overlapping the corners.

Place Lucy and the bears in the top pocket and her clothes in the bottom. The quilt may be folded in thirds and will fit in the large pocket on the right. Place Felicity's clothes on hangers and tie a piece of narrow ribbon around the two buttons on the front of the wardrobe to close it.

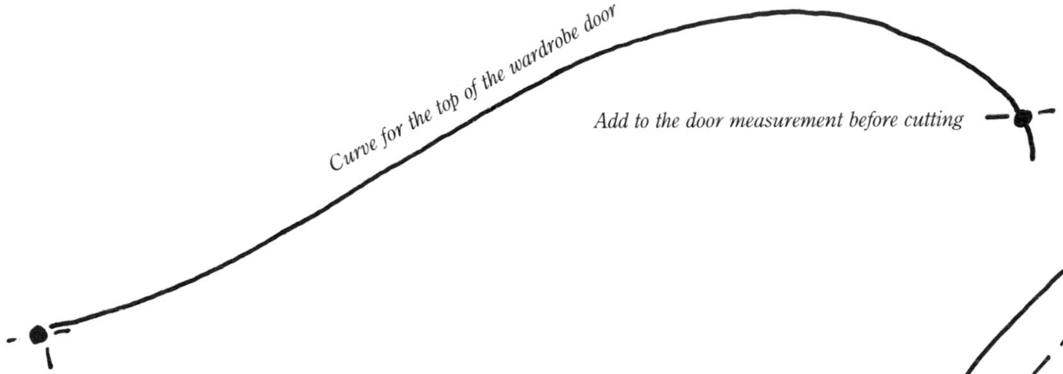

Curve for the top of the wardrobe door

Add to the door measurement before cutting

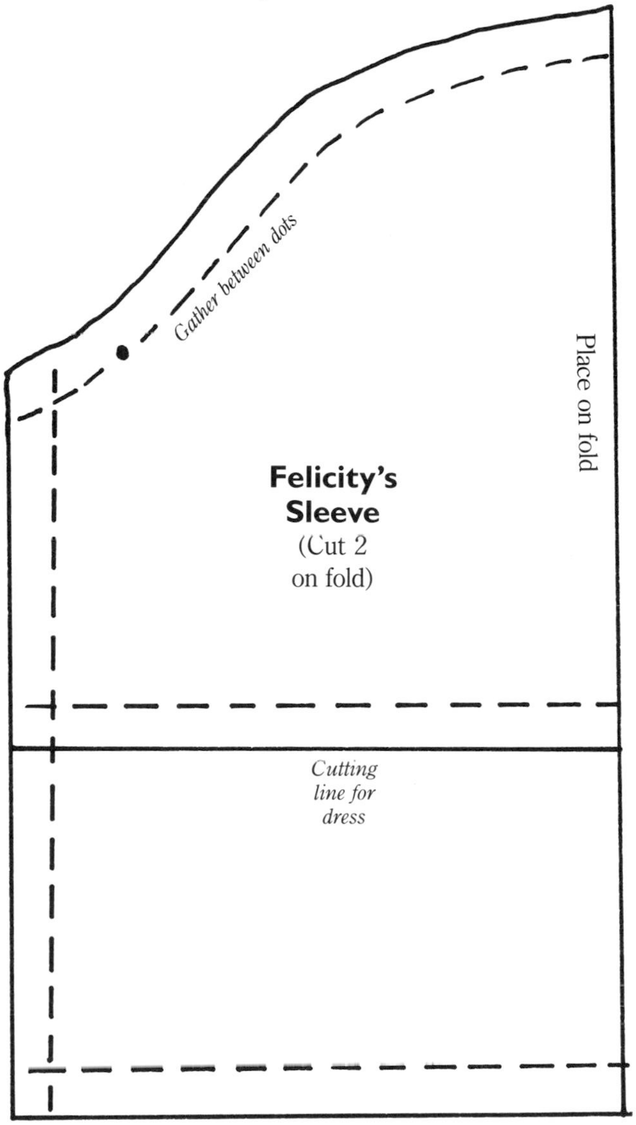

Paint black shoe

Place on fold

Gather between dots

Felicity's Sleeve

(Cut 2 on fold)

Cutting line for dress

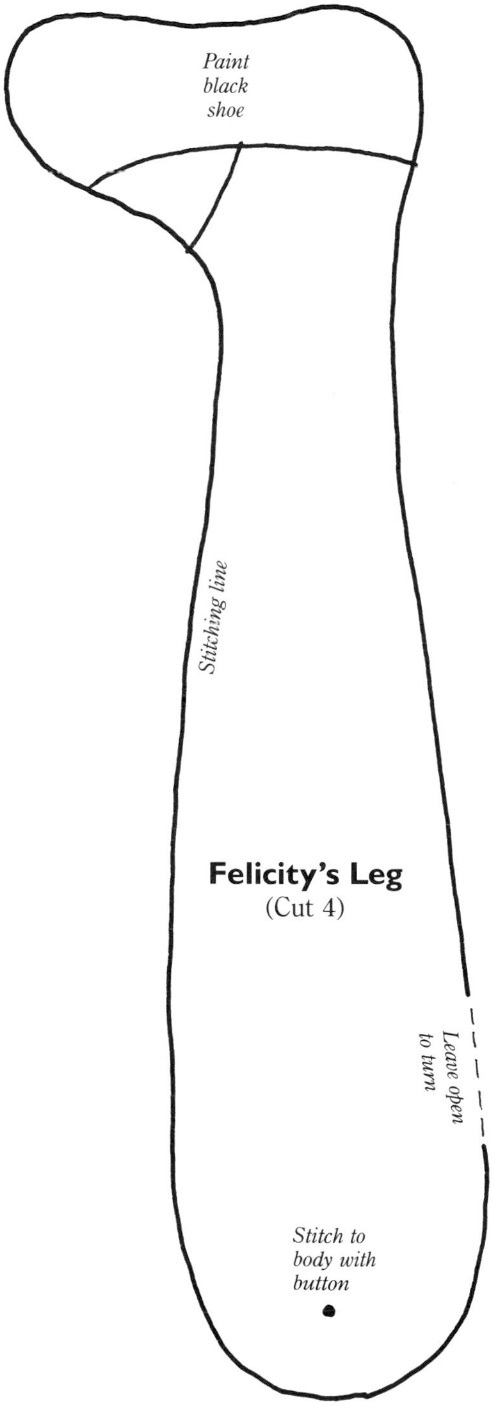

Stitching line

Felicity's Leg

(Cut 4)

Leave open to turn

Stitch to body with button

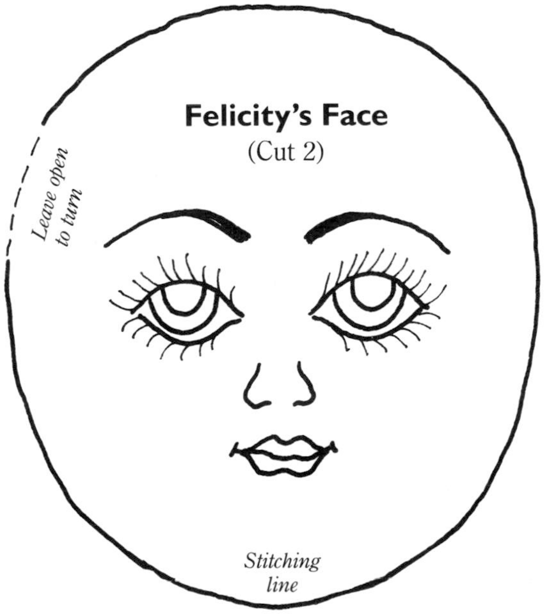

Leave open to turn

Felicity's Face

(Cut 2)

Stitching line

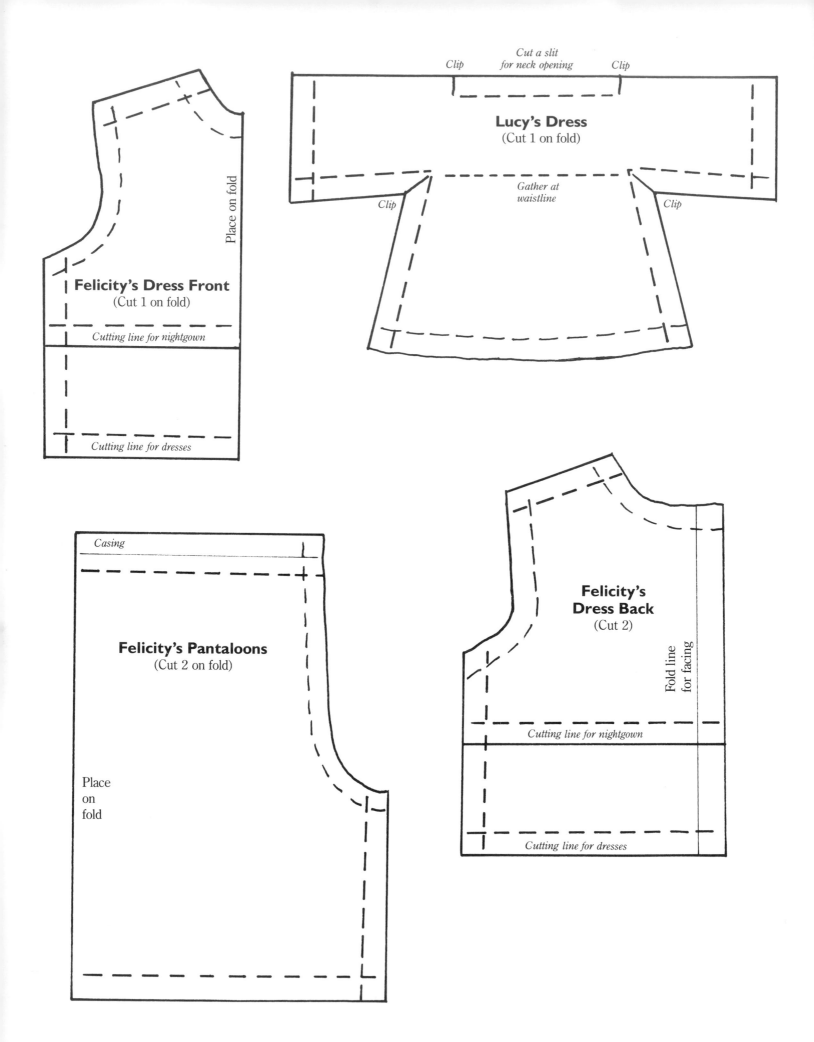

Lucy's Dress
(Cut 1 on fold)

Cut a slit for neck opening

Clip

Clip

Clip

Clip

Gather at waistline

Felicity's Dress Front
(Cut 1 on fold)

Place on fold

Cutting line for nightgown

Cutting line for dresses

Felicity's Pantaloons
(Cut 2 on fold)

Casing

Place on fold

Felicity's Dress Back
(Cut 2)

Fold line for facing

Cutting line for nightgown

Cutting line for dresses

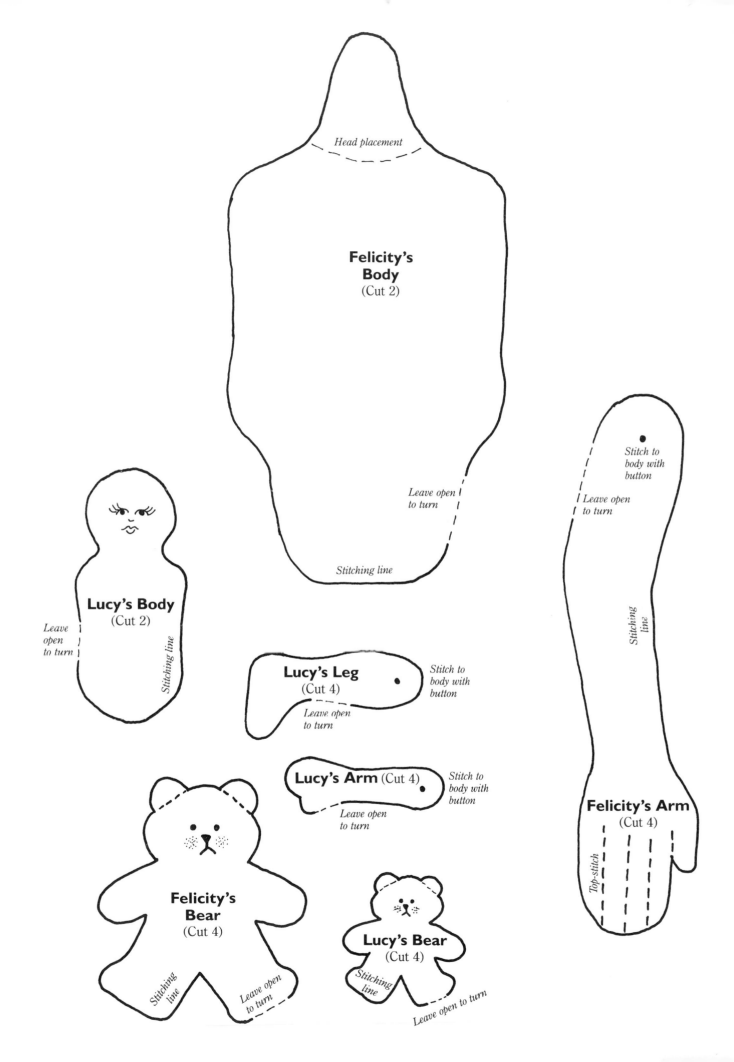

Felicity's Body (Cut 2)

Head placement

Leave open to turn

Stitching line

Stitch to body with button

Leave open to turn

Stitching line

Felicity's Arm (Cut 4)

Top-stitch

Lucy's Body (Cut 2)

Leave open to turn

Stitching line

Lucy's Leg (Cut 4)

Stitch to body with button

Leave open to turn

Lucy's Arm (Cut 4)

Stitch to body with button

Leave open to turn

Felicity's Bear (Cut 4)

Stitching line

Leave open to turn

Lucy's Bear (Cut 4)

Stitching line

Leave open to turn

Romantic
BERNADETTE AND MARGUERITE

by Miriam Gourley

About four years ago, I designed a very tall, slender doll whom I called Chloe. She was dressed in 1920's clothing, her hair was painted and she was very mannequin-like. I wanted to use this style of body but dress her differently for this book. I wanted to design the romantic doll for this book—and made two because I couldn't decide which color scheme I liked better.

I'm a rather eclectic person. I avoid decorating my home with objects that match. I like Modigliani prints, floral chintz, country antiques, southwest art, some Victorian decorating ideas and some modern elements. That is also my approach to dollmaking and other designing challenges. I dress in a style that I call "Funky Victorian," and that is probably a good description for the dress style of these dolls. There are elements of Victorian style (lace and roses), yet the cut of the clothes is reminiscent of the 1920's. The spangly tulle and gold-edged wired ribbon are the funky elements.

Bernadette and Marguerite are named after two important people in my life. Bernadette was one of my best friends in the first grade. She was a beautiful brown-eyed girl with very long hair who remained my friend throughout high school. Marguerite is my mother's name—my mother the school teacher, the farmer's wife, the student of French and Spanish, artist, mother of eight, my mentor and friend. It was easy to name the dolls. After all, these romantic names fit the dolls. I didn't realize until later, however, that these dolls should be French hatmakers. I was inspired to give them this occupation when I saw a wonderful doll-sized cupboard in a doll museum: the cupboard was filled with all sorts of trims and laces, and it had a tiny hatbox sitting on the counter. I knew that Marguerite and Bernadette would be at home in that kind of environment; as I began making their hats, they enjoyed the process so much I knew they were telling me I was right.

MATERIALS LIST (for one doll)

1/3 yard of muslin for the torso, the head and the boots
1/3 yard of solid or print for the legs
1/4 yard of fabric for the jacket and the hat
1/4 yard of fabric for the jacket lining and the hat lining
1/4 yard of fabric for the blouse
1/3 yard of fabric for the skirt
11-1/2″ of antique crocheted lace 2-1/2″ to 3″ wide
1/2-ounce package of natural-curl mohair
Sulky® Iron-On Transfer pen (black)
Fabric fixative (such as Sta-Set)
Delta Fabric Paints in the following colors:
   “Gleams” Pearl Finish, “Gleams” Violet Pearl, “Gleams”
   Blue Pearl, Starlite Dye (Brown), Fabric Dye (Black and
   Light Brown) and Glitter Stuff (Crystal)
24 small silver beads (for the boots)
Metallic thread (for quilting the jackets)
16″ × 20″ piece of thin cotton/polyester batting
Small glass beads (optional)
Cording for edges of the quilted jacket and the hat (optional)
Gold rope or tulle for the sash around the jacket
Hat embellishments: ribbon, lace or floral accessories

CONSTRUCTION

Body

1. Read B2 and transfer the face (see B6) and use the Sulky® iron-on transfer pen to apply the facial detail.

2. Stitch the head together and stuff according to the suggestions at E3.

3. Apply the cheek color according to the directions at C4, then paint the facial details.

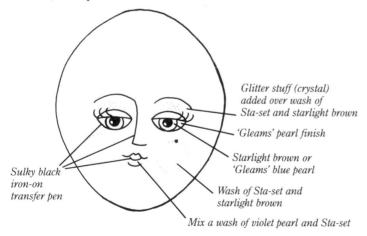

Glitter stuff (crystal) added over wash of Sta-set and starlight brown

'Gleams' pearl finish

Starlight brown or 'Gleams' blue pearl

Sulky black iron-on transfer pen

Wash of Sta-set and starlight brown

Mix a wash of violet pearl and Sta-set

4. Cut out all the other body pieces (see B2). Use tracing paper to transfer the lower bootline to the boot piece.

5. Follow instructions at E1 through E5 (Step B). Paint the lower part of the boot black and the upper section white.

6. When the paint is dry, stitch small silver beads on the boot front seams to imitate small buttons. Use a fairly sturdy needle, but one that will still fit through the hole of the bead, and stitch the beads 3/8″ to 1/4″ apart down the white section of the boot. You will use approximately 12 beads per foot.

7. Attach the head according to the directions at E11. Construct the hair according to the instructions at F6 (Steps 1-8, 10 and 12).

Clothes

1. Construct the blouse according to G5 (Steps 1-5 and 7-11).

2. Follow the directions at G6 to make the skirt.

3. The doll's jacket may be made according to the directions at G7.

4. I encourage you to find your own way of finishing the doll—use a favorite antique button as a belt buckle or a piece of brocade from Aunt Mabel's antique dress.

Hat

1. To create the hat, place the hat pieces with the right sides together and stitch around the curved edge. Repeat this step for the lining.

Trim the seams to 1/8″ and place the hat and the lining with the right sides together.

2. Stitch around the bottom edge and leave a 2″ opening for turning the hat.

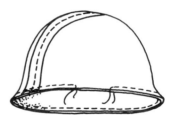

3. Turn the hat right side out and press the edges. Stitch the opening closed. Fold up one of the edges for the front side.

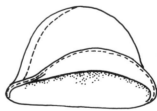

Trim the hat as you wish. When applying embellishments, many designers find odd numbers give better visual balance than even numbers. Cording may be stitched to the edge of the hat as I have done on the blue hat. The blue hat also has three ribbon roses nestled into the folds of a small ribbon fan. The other hat has three ribbon roses on a looped ribbon base. All these embellishment ideas are on pages 42-43.

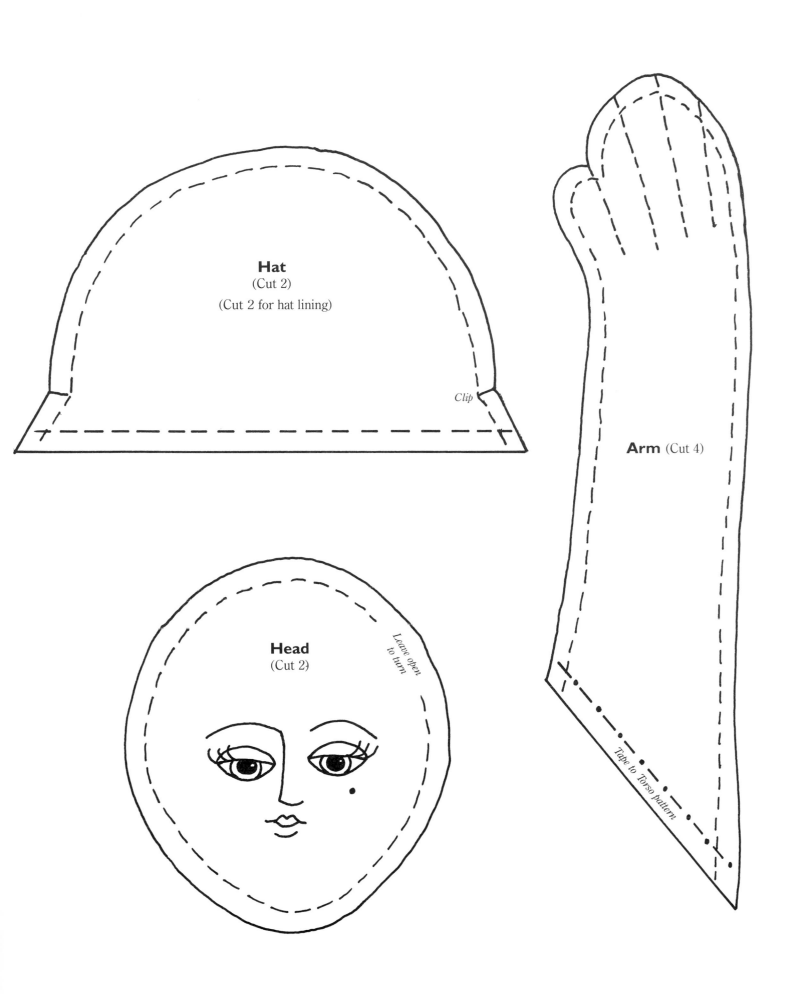

Hat
(Cut 2)

(Cut 2 for hat lining)

Clip

Arm (Cut 4)

Head
(Cut 2)

Leave open to turn

Tape to Torso pattern

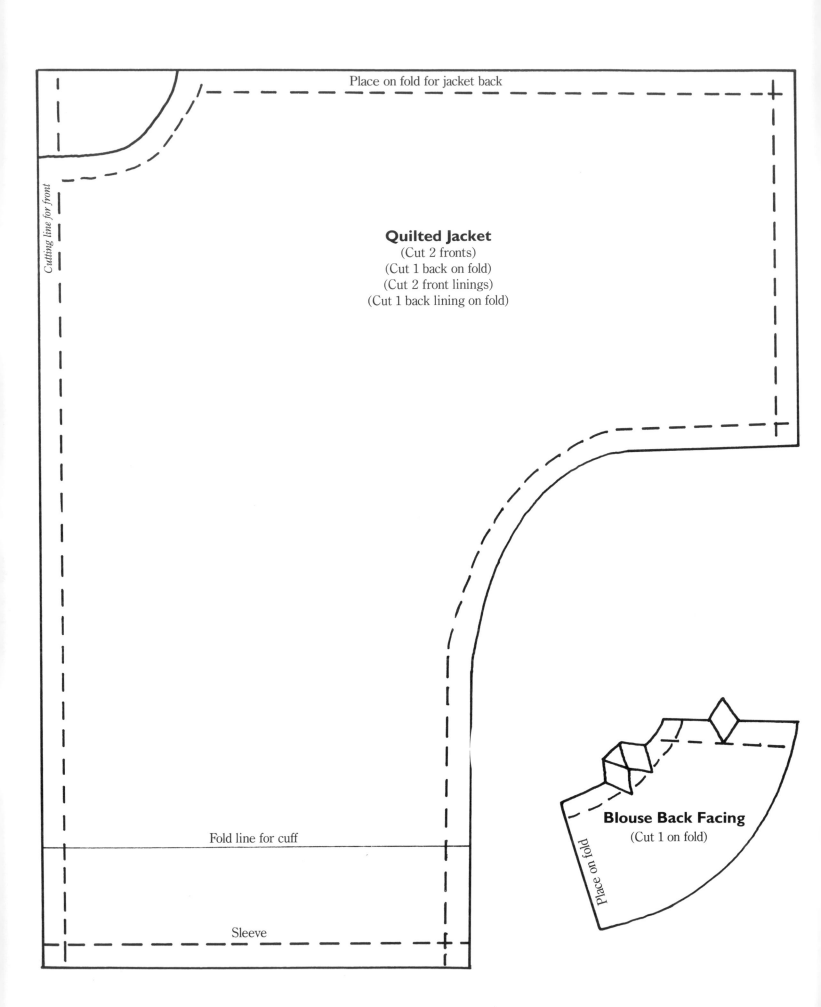

Place on fold for jacket back

Cutting line for front

Quilted Jacket
(Cut 2 fronts)
(Cut 1 back on fold)
(Cut 2 front linings)
(Cut 1 back lining on fold)

Fold line for cuff

Sleeve

Blouse Back Facing
(Cut 1 on fold)

Place on fold

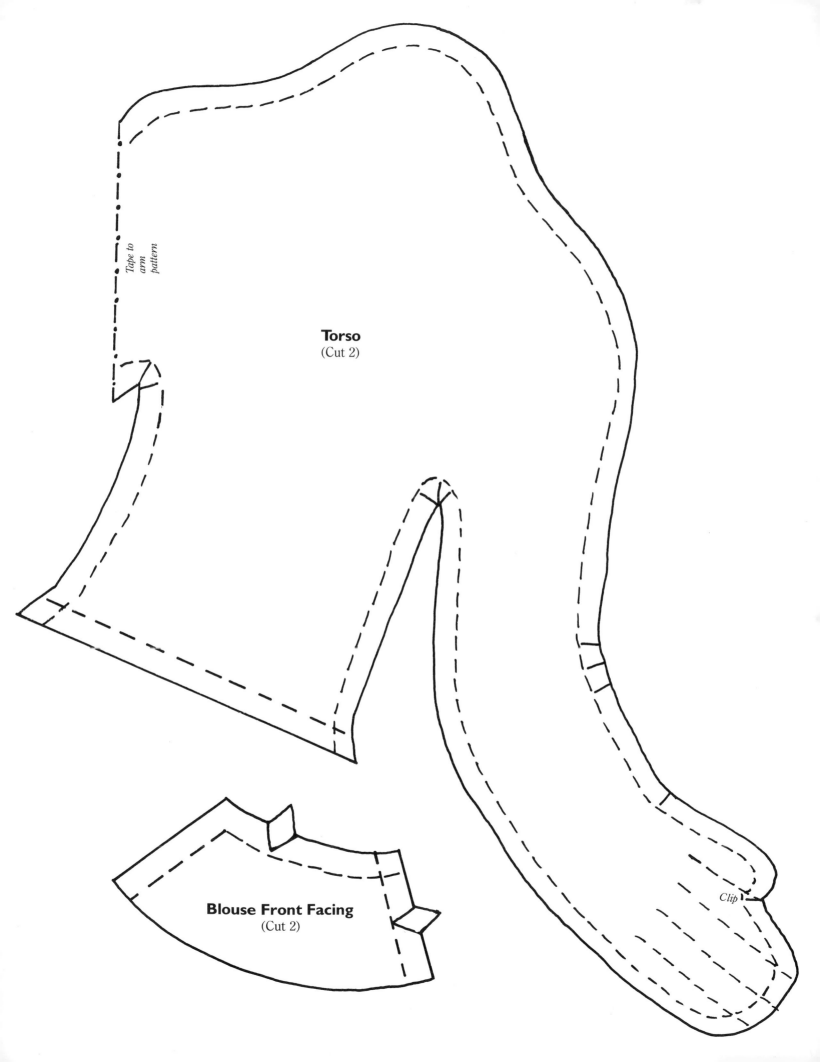

Torso
(Cut 2)

Tape to arm pattern

Clip

Blouse Front Facing
(Cut 2)

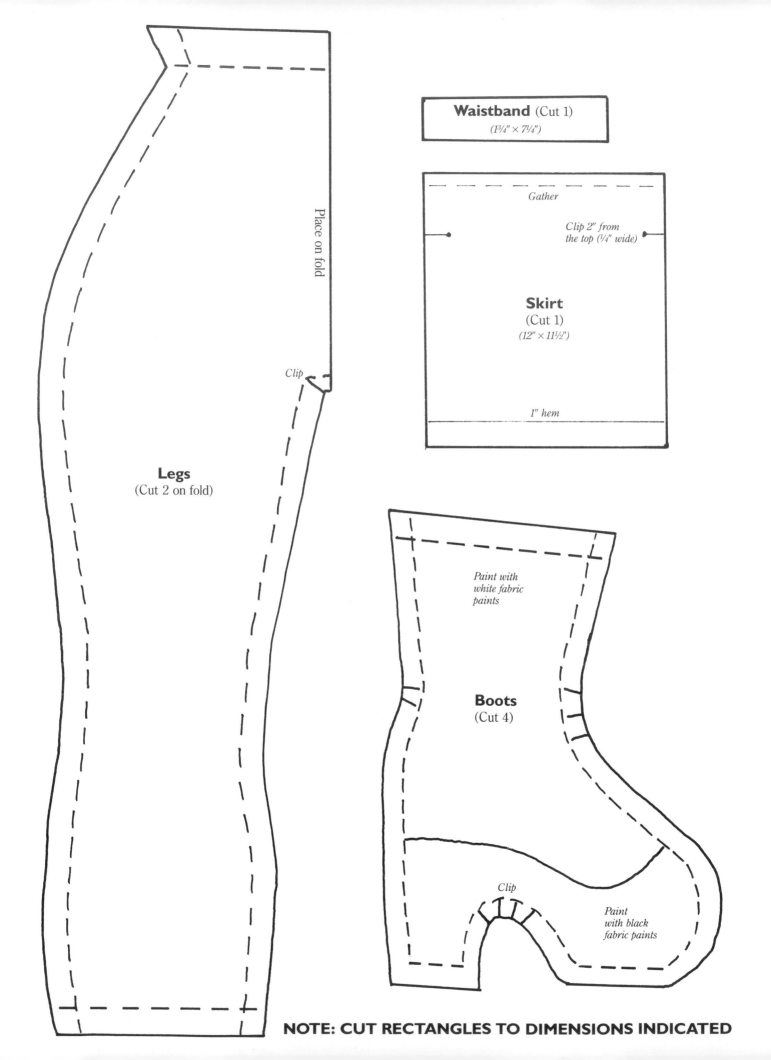

Waistband (Cut 1)
(1¾" × 7¼")

Gather

*Clip 2" from
the top (¼" wide)*

Skirt
(Cut 1)
(12" × 11½")

1" hem

Place on fold

Clip

Legs
(Cut 2 on fold)

*Paint with
white fabric
paints*

Boots
(Cut 4)

Clip

*Paint
with black
fabric paints*

NOTE: CUT RECTANGLES TO DIMENSIONS INDICATED

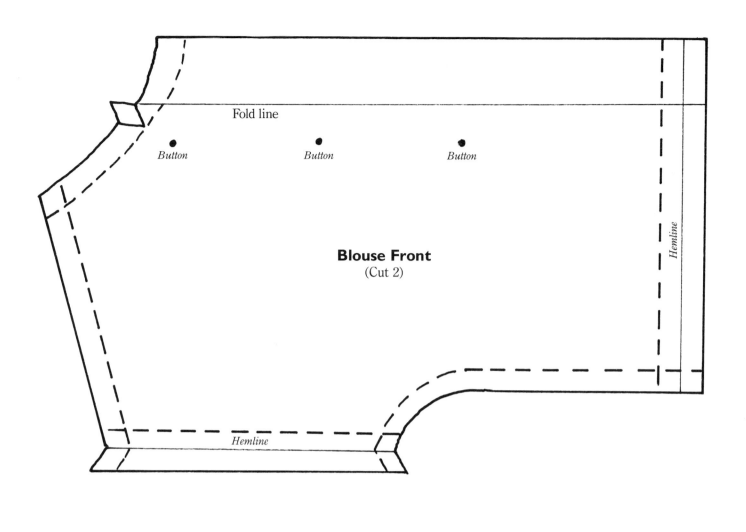

Fold line

Button   Button   Button

Blouse Front
(Cut 2)

Hemline

Hemline

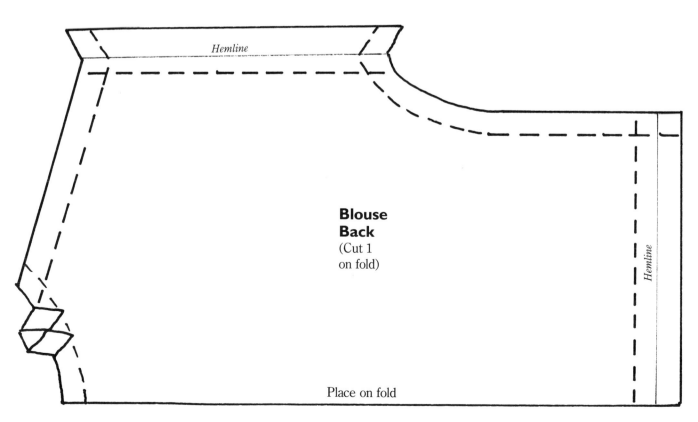

Hemline

**Blouse
Back**
(Cut 1
on fold)

Hemline

Place on fold

Whimsical
PROFESSOR HOLLY BEETLE

by Ruth Landis

Ruth Kuykendall Landis is a native northern Californian with family roots throughout the Southwest. She received a degree in art from California State University—Sacramento, where she studied and exhibited paintings, sculpture, ceramics and fiber arts. Starting with craft fairs, Ruth progressed to designing original dolls and quilts for her pattern company, which is called On the Edge Designs. She enjoys teaching classes and the challenges of creating dolls and quilts with a touch of whimsy. Ruth lives in Sacramento with her husband, Tony, and their three daughters, Andie, Ali and Adie.

"Whimsical" is the word that best describes Ruth's work. She likes to make dolls that embody her sense of humor. Sometimes she takes the approach of working with opposites. For example, she enjoyed using the deep purple and yellow combination. She carefully selected appropriate colors to give the appearance of antique clothing. She doesn't usually use pure colors: Ruth likes the look of subdued colors. You will also notice the combination of opposites in her choice of fabric types—velvets used with cotton, and small prints with plaids.

Ruth also enjoys using common materials in uncommon ways. She wanted to find a new way of using yarn for hair. Her final result was made by winding the yarn around the doll's head, then hardening it. This process was borrowed from a method called "poor man's porcelain," which is a way of creating a cloth doll and hardening her face to resemble porcelain. This process was similar to the concept of floor cloth, which was canvas painted to resemble the more expensive hand-made carpets that only the wealthy could afford.

Professor Holly Beetle was named after a good friend of Ruth's, who used to lament her last name. She looked forward to the day she would marry and change her last name, but said that if marriage eluded her, she would become a professor to give her name more dignity. Holly was Ruth's fellow art student. Ruth said the doll's hard body made her think of a beetle. Hence, Professor Beetle acquired her name.

MATERIALS LIST

1/2 yard of bleached muslin for the body
1/2 yard of cotton fabric for the dress
1/4 yard of velveteen for the overskirt and the cap sleeves
1/4 yard of cotton fabric for the facings and the piping
1/4 yard of cotton fabric for the jacket
1/4 yard of cotton fabric for the jacket lining and the dress waistband
Scrap of fabric for the tie
Scrap of lace to edge the top of the boots
1/2″ antique button for the tie
Yarn for the hair
Powder blush
Embroidery floss (black and red)
Fabric paint (white and black)
Mod Podge® or another water-base sealer

CONSTRUCTION

Body

1. Follow the instructions at B1 and B4 or B5. Proceed with instructions at E3 (Steps 2-3).

2. Stuff the doll, noting the directions at E4, E5 (Step B) and E6.

3. After the arms have been stuffed, attach them to the torso as instructed at E17 (Step 4).

4. Sculpt the nose according to the directions at E10.

5. Embroider the eyes and the mouth as indicated.

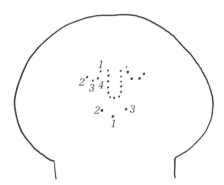

6. Wind the yarn onto the head, noting the instructions at F10.

7. Dilute the Mod Podge® (one part of Mod Podge® to one part water) and paint the feet, face, head and hair to the lines indicated on the pattern. Make sure all the areas are thoroughly covered with the mixture, as this step seals the fabric. Allow the doll to dry completely.

8. Color the cheeks with powder blush. If you wish to stain or color the face, do it now. Use a very small brush and paint in the white areas of the eyes.

9. Re-paint the face, hair and feet with the Mod Podge® mixture and allow it to dry. Repeat this procedure until the painted areas are smooth and shiny.

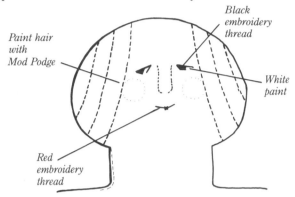

Paint hair with Mod Podge

Black embroidery thread

White paint

Red embroidery thread

Use a single strand for mouth and eyes.

10. Paint the feet with the black fabric paint and allow it to dry. Add one more coat of black paint.

11. Glue lace around the upper edges of the boots.

Dress

1. Cut out the dress and assemble it, noting the instructions at G3 (Steps 1, 2C, 9-12 and 15C). Place the sleeves with the right sides together, stitch them and turn them right sides out. Stitch to the bodice as illustrated at Step 4B.

2. Finish the skirt hems by using the contrasting fabric to face the upper skirt instead of hemming it. The same contrasting fabric may be used to bind the under skirt. (see page 44 for binding instructions).

Jacket

1. Make 36″ of piping according to the directions on page 44.

2. Place the jacket pattern on the fabric which has been folded with the right sides together. Cut out the jacket and repeat the procedure for the lining. Use your zipper foot and machine baste the piping to the sleeve edges, the neck and the back edges of the jacket. Place the sleeve facing and the jacket sleeve with the right sides together (the piping sandwiched between the facing and the sleeve).

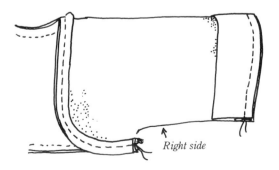

Right side

Use the zipper foot to stitch the facing to the piping and the jacket. Press the raw edges toward the facing. Fold the jacket sleeves together, matching the notches, and stitch the underarm seam.

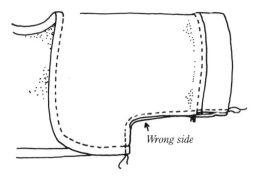

Wrong side

Clip the curves and press the seams open. Repeat these steps for the lining, omitting the facing. Place the lining and the jacket with the right sides together and use the zipper foot to stitch through all the layers next to the basting stitch around the neckline and back edge of the jacket. Leave a 2″

opening for turning. Be sure to catch the raw edges of the piping in the seam so they don't show after you turn the jacket. Turn the jacket right side out through the opening and press it. Stitch the opening closed by hand and press the sleeve facings under 1/4″. Fold the facings up to cover the raw edges of the sleeve and piping. Hand stitch them in place.

Necktie

Fold the necktie in half lengthwise and stitch around the edges, leaving a 1″ opening. Clip the corners and turn the tie right side out. Press it and place it around the doll's neck. Tie it in the standard manner (you may need some male assistance). Stitch the antique button midway down the tie.

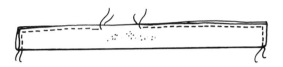

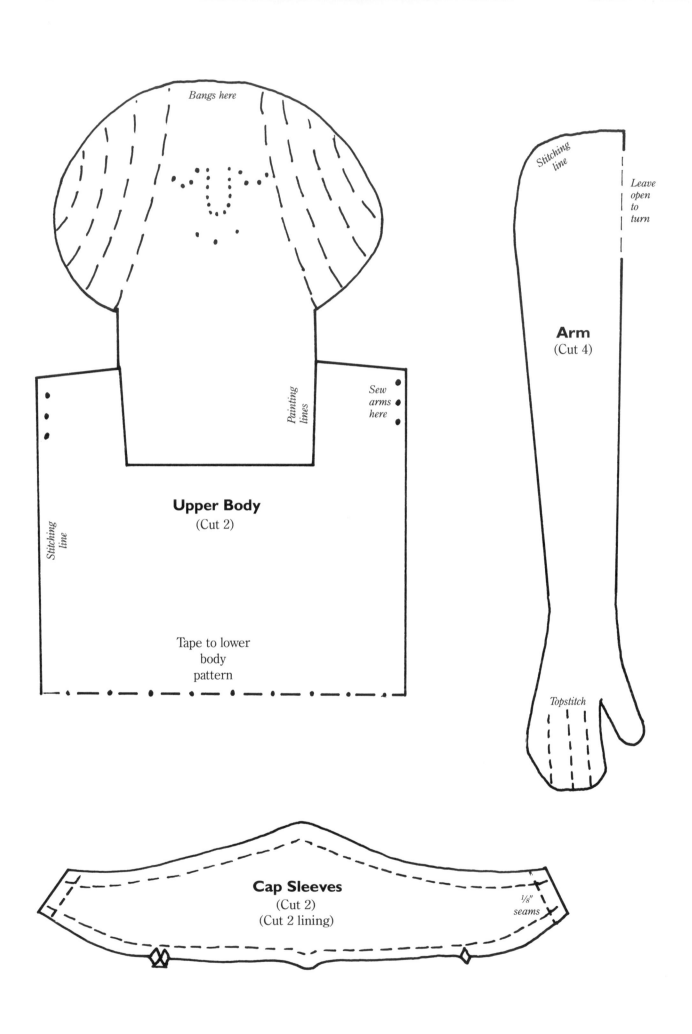

Bangs here

Stitching line

Leave open to turn

Arm
(Cut 4)

Painting lines

Sew arms here

Upper Body
(Cut 2)

Stitching line

Tape to lower
body
pattern

Topstitch

Cap Sleeves
(Cut 2)
(Cut 2 lining)

⅛″
seams

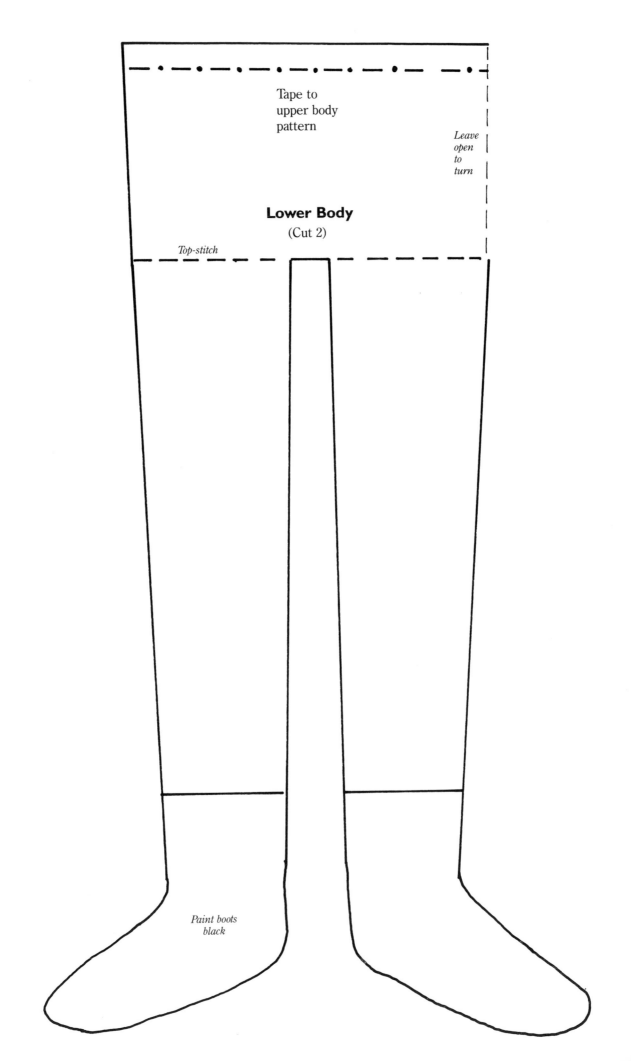

Tape to
upper body
pattern

*Leave
open
to
turn*

Lower Body
(Cut 2)

Top-stitch

*Paint boots
black*

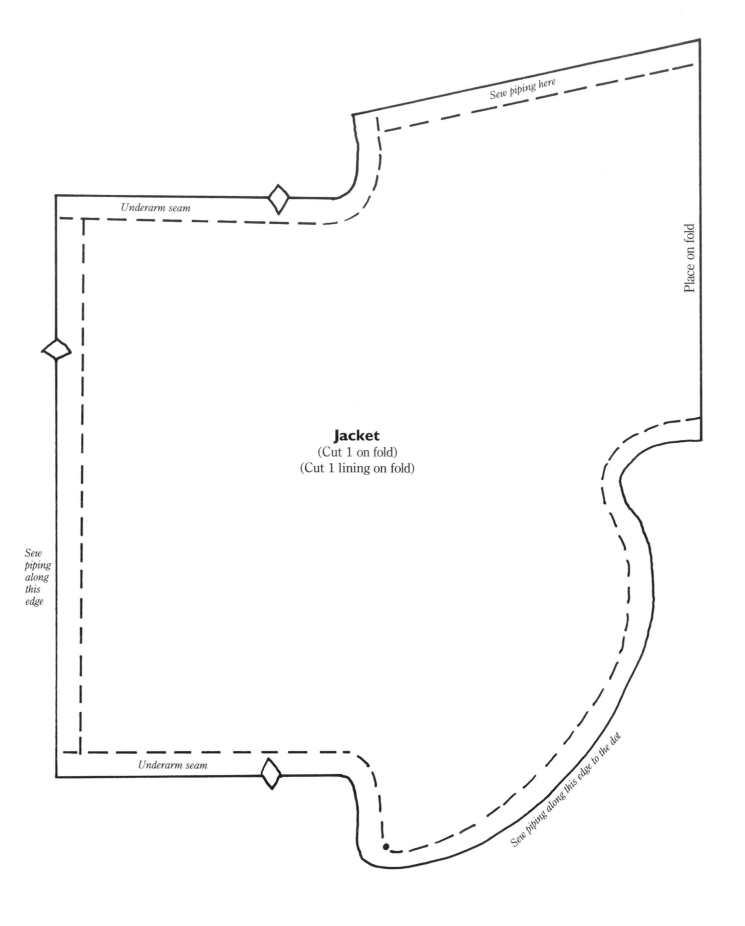

Sew piping here

Underarm seam

Place on fold

Jacket
(Cut 1 on fold)
(Cut 1 lining on fold)

Sew
piping
along
this
edge

Underarm seam

Sew piping along this edge to the dot

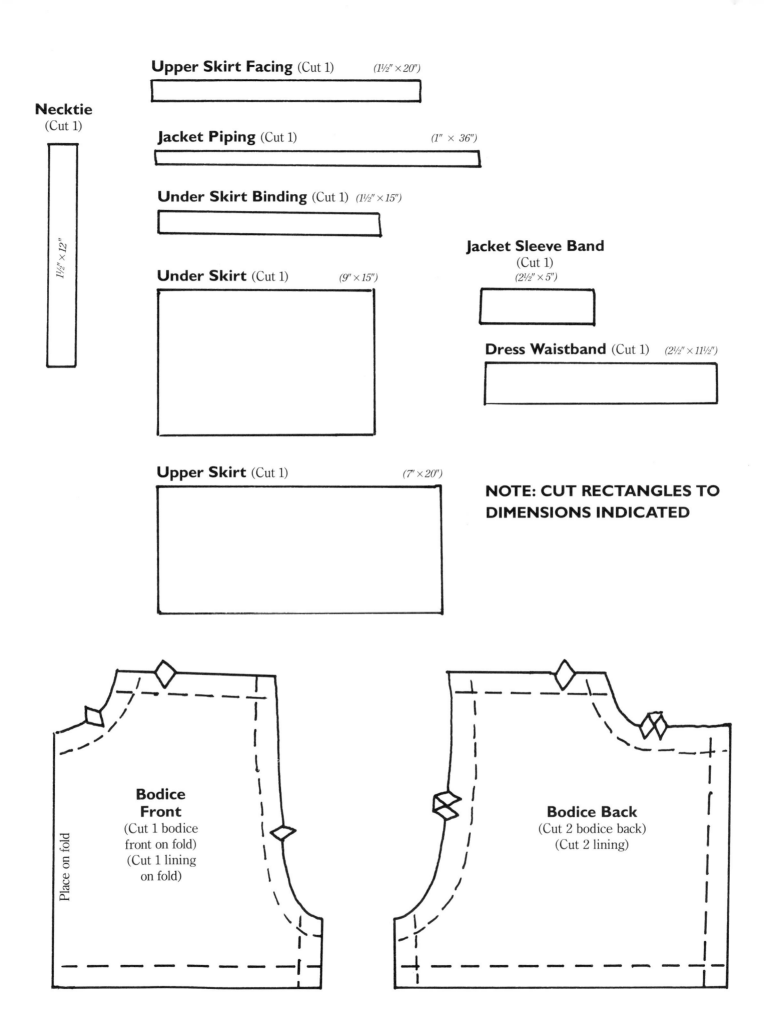

Upper Skirt Facing (Cut 1) *(1½" × 20")*

Jacket Piping (Cut 1) *(1" × 36")*

Under Skirt Binding (Cut 1) *(1½" × 15")*

Necktie
(Cut 1)

1½" × 12"

Under Skirt (Cut 1) *(9" × 15")*

Jacket Sleeve Band
(Cut 1)
(2½" × 5")

Dress Waistband (Cut 1) *(2½" × 11½")*

Upper Skirt (Cut 1) *(7" × 20")*

NOTE: CUT RECTANGLES TO DIMENSIONS INDICATED

**Bodice
Front**
(Cut 1 bodice
front on fold)
(Cut 1 lining
on fold)

Place on fold

Bodice Back
(Cut 2 bodice back)
(Cut 2 lining)

Patriotic
DIRK

by Margaret Peters

When I first began designing patterns, Margaret was representing several design companies and agreed to include my designs. As I became acquainted with her, I discovered that besides her countless adventure stories, Margaret is very patriotic. Her trademark is anything red, white and blue and she dresses (and looks stunning) in these colors.

A few years ago, Margaret designed an angel in red, white and blue. She made several more and decorated a Christmas tree which is now in the Smithsonian Institution in Washington, D.C. Margaret has designed several dolls and one-of-a-kind quilted garments which have been displayed in special exhibits. She has also co-ordinated an exhibit of flags to celebrate America's 200th birthday.

Margaret wanted to do a doll commemorating the brave soldiers of the American Revolution. Her doll, Dirk, is a young flag bearer for his regiment. He has paused to re-tie his leggings, being mindful not to let the flag touch the ground. While keeping a sharp lookout, he thinks of his sweetheart, Peggy, who is back home. Dirk recalls the day he left: Peggy gave him the ribbon from her hair and tied it around his, as a token of her love.

MATERIALS LIST

1/2 yard of flesh-colored cotton for the body
1/4 yard of small print or stripe for the shirt
1/4 yard of dark cotton for the pants
1/8 yard of unbleached muslin
6″ × 8″ piece of soft leather or Ultrasuede® for the vest
1 package curly wool crepe for the hair
Fine-tip permanent-ink marking pen (brown)
Colored pencils for the eyes and mouth (light red and blue)
Fabric paint (black) for the shoes
Three 1/4″-wide white buttons for the shirt
One 3/8″ black button for the pants
6″ × 9″ pine board for the base
Sphagnum moss to cover the base (optional)
4″ × 6″ American flag on pole
Black buttonhole twist or carpet thread for the laces in the shoes
1 yard of jute or twine (to wind around the leggings)
Scrap of 1/8″ blue ribbon

CONSTRUCTION

Body

1. Follow directions for B1. Use a #2 pencil to outline the facial features lightly. Complete the body assembly by following directions at E3 (Steps 2-3). Proceed with E4.

2. Follow the directions at E5.

3. Continue at E6 and E9 to stuff the leg firmly up to 3″ from the bottom of the foot, then top-stitch to form the knee. Stuff the leg to within 1/2″ of the top edge. Insert the arms into the shoulder and the legs into the body with the feet pointing forward. Follow the guidelines at E15. Pencil the shoe outline onto the lower part of the leg. Paint the shoes with black fabric paint and allow it to dry thoroughly.

4. Thread a needle with buttonhole twist or carpet thread and lace the shoe.

5. Leave the ends of the thread long enough to tie into a bow, and clip off the excess.

6. Use the brown fine-tip permanent-ink marking pen to trace the features. Use the seam to keep the face centered. Color the iris of the eyes with the blue pencil. Use the light-red pencil to color the mouth. Color the cheeks by applying powdered blush with a cotton swab.

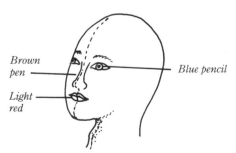

7. Cut two 3″ pieces of curly crepe hair. Unbraid them and loosen the hair fiber. Apply it to the doll's head, as instructed in F11.

Vest

1. Cut the vest pattern from leather or Ultrasuede®. Make tailor tacks on one side of the vest to indicate pocket placement (see B3).

2. Pin the pocket to the vest and stitch the pocket very close to the sides and the bottom edges.

3. Stitch the shoulder and the side seams using a very simple lapped technique.

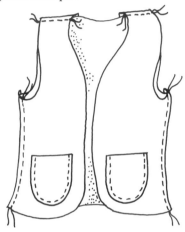

Shirt

1. Gather one 7″ edge of the sleeve piece, starting and finishing 1/2″ from the edge. At the opposite end, begin and finish the gathering stitch 1/4″ from the edges.

2. With the right sides together, stitch the shoulder seams of the front and back of the shirt.

3. With the right sides together, stitch the facing pieces together at the shoulder seams. Press all the seams open.

4. Fold the collar piece in half lengthwise, with the right sides together. Use a 1/8″ seam allowance and stitch across each end. Trim the corners, turn it right side out and press it.

5. Pin the collar to the right side of the shirt. The collar is set in 1/8″ from the front edges of the shirt. Baste it in place.

6. With the right sides together, pin the facing around the neckline and front of the shirt. Use a 1/4″ seam allowance and stitch from the bottom edge of the shirt up the front, around the neck and down the other side. Clip the corners near the collar. Before turning, stitch across the bottom of the front facings and zig zag the bottom edge. Clip the bottom corners of the facing. Turn the facings to the inside of the shirt.

7. Gather the sleeve edge which has been stitched 1/4″ from the edges to fit the sleeve cuff. With the right sides together, stitch the cuff to the sleeve.

8. Pin the sleeve to the shoulder of the shirt, with the right sides together, adjusting the gathers. Stitch it to the shirt.

9. With the right sides of the shirt together, stitch from the cuffs to the bottom edge of the shirt.

10. Fold up the cuffs to cover the raw edges of the lower sleeves and hand stitch them. Turn the shirt right side out.

11. Press up the hem and machine stitch it in place.

12. Sew on the buttons, place the shirt on the doll and overlap the front edges. Stitch the shirt closed.

Pants

1. Cut out the pants pieces. Cut a 7" × 1-1/4" piece for the waistband.

2. Stitch the front center seam, clip it and press it toward the left side. Top-stitch the fly, fold the pants with the right sides together and stitch the back seam.

3. Fold the waistband in half lengthwise and stitch both ends. Turn it right side out and press it.

4. Pin the waistband to the top edge of the pants with the raw edges together. Overlap the front left waistband over the right side.

5. Stitch around the waist and press the raw edges toward the pants.

6. Sew the 3/8" button on the waistband.

7. With the right sides together, stitch up the leg seam from ankle to ankle. Turn the pants right side out and put them on the doll. You will not need to hem the pants, because the leggings will be wrapped around the raw edges.

8. When the doll is dressed, tear another piece of muslin 1" × 12". Cut it in half and wrap each half around each leg to form leggings. Secure the leggings by wrapping them with jute or twine. Tie a knot at the top.

Finishing

Dirk can be placed on a doll stand or sit tying his leggings. To seat him, paint the board with a light coat of white glue and press the moss into it. Allow the glue to dry thoroughly, then hot glue the doll to the base. Bend one leg up, as pictured, and hot glue the foot to the base. Put the jute into the doll's hands and glue his fingers around the jute to secure it. Insert the flag on the pole between his right arm and the side of his body and use hot glue to position the pole.

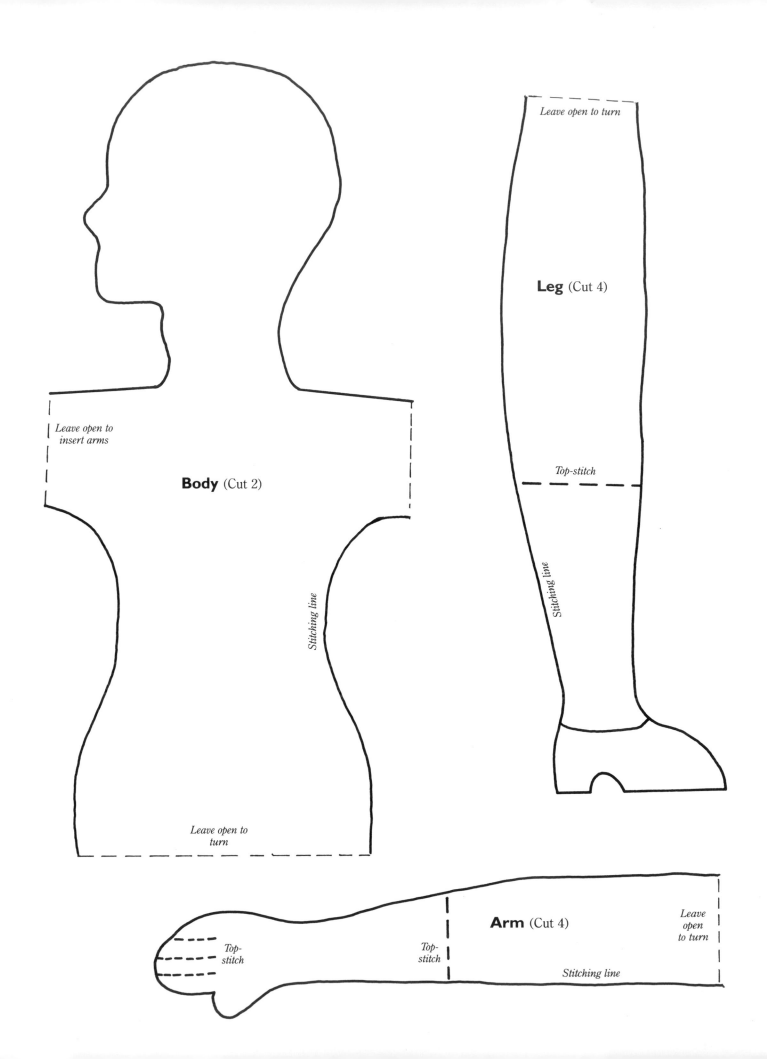

Body (Cut 2)

Leave open to insert arms

Leave open to turn

Stitching line

Leg (Cut 4)

Leave open to turn

Top-stitch

Stitching line

Arm (Cut 4)

Leave open to turn

Top-stitch

Top-stitch

Stitching line

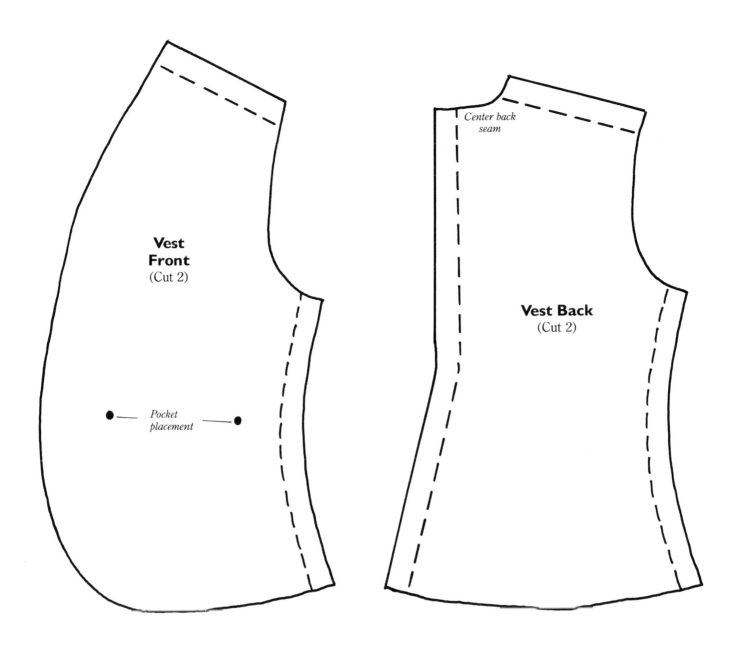

**Vest
Front**
(Cut 2)

● Pocket
placement ●

*Center back
seam*

Vest Back
(Cut 2)

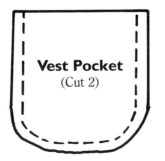

Vest Pocket
(Cut 2)

Country
REBECCA ANN

by Susie Robbins

Susie Robbins's dolls are full of personality. She believes that once you construct the "bare bones" of the doll, your personality should be evident in the rest of the construction process and especially in the clothing. Susie envelops her dolls in wonderful costumes, sometimes with glitzy embellishments and sometimes with rustic accessories and fabrics. Rebecca Ann was first dressed in the country clothing and hat, then Susie created an heirloom doll by using old kitchen towels, antique table linens and old jewelry. We see that, by changing the fabric, accessories and hair color, the dollmaker creates a new look for the doll.

Susie's designs fall into two categories: commercial patterns and one-of-a-kind dolls. When she designs patterns, she must know her audience—their skill level, interests and current focus. Many times, she creates a series of dolls; she created a wizard, which was the first in a series called "The Keeper of Legends." Creating one-of-a-kind designs is something which she isn't able to do often but what stimulates all designers to be more creative: there are no patterns to make and to re-cut until the pieces are just right, no restrictions or an audience to please.

Susie says it is necessary only to show students how to put the pieces together. Once the body has been constructed, the clothing tells the real story, and she encourages her students to be very creative. Susie cites the following example: "I like thinking about the mother of seven boys who took a class from me to make a bear. This woman made the bear's coat from the skirt she wore when she graduated from high school. Tears—real splashing tears—came to her eyes when she came to class the second week saying, 'I never thought I could do something like this.' Such are the real rewards of a dollmaker and teacher."

Rebecca Ann is the name of Susie's daughter, who was named for her fraternal grandparents, Rebecca and Ananias. Susie cherished how much love these two grandparents had for their family and how appreciated they were.

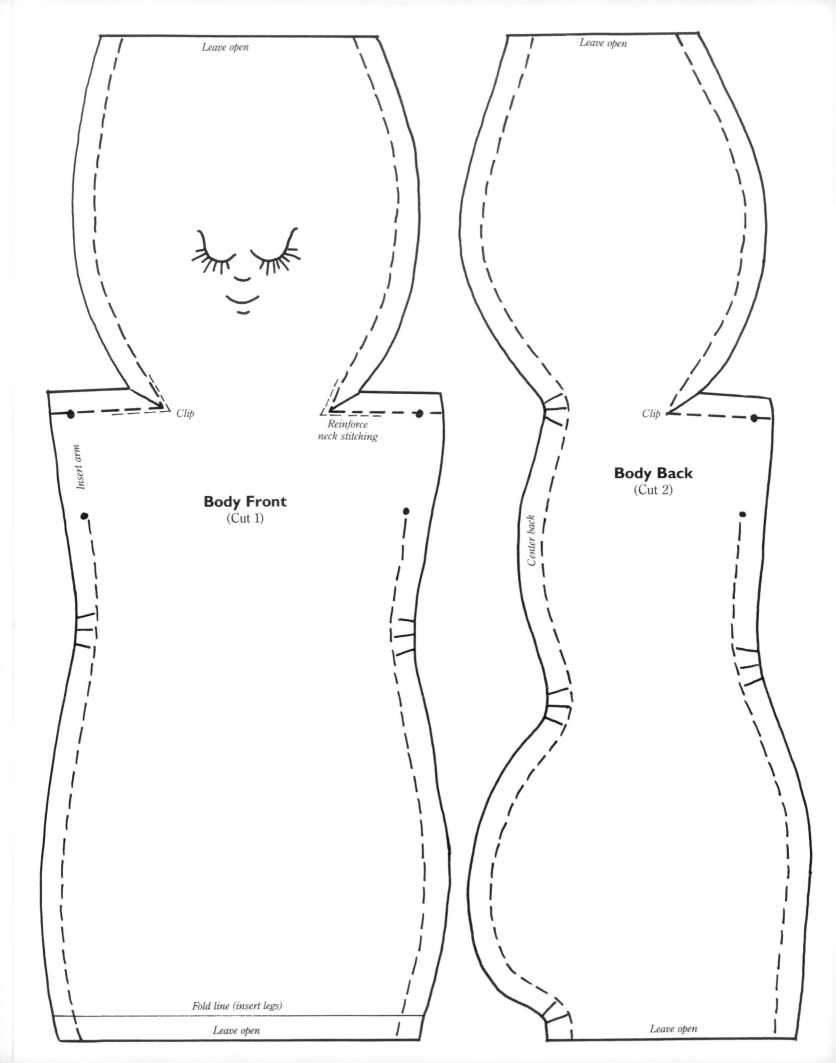

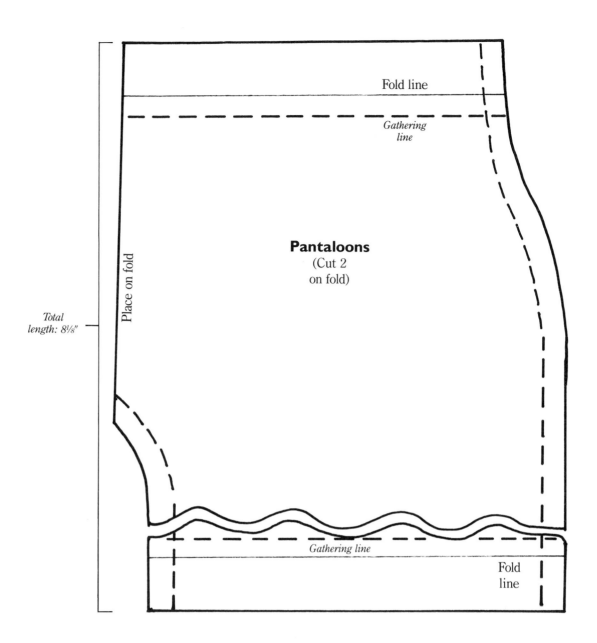

Fold line

*Gathering
line*

Pantaloons
(Cut 2
on fold)

Place on fold

*Total
length: 8⅛″*

Gathering line

Fold
line

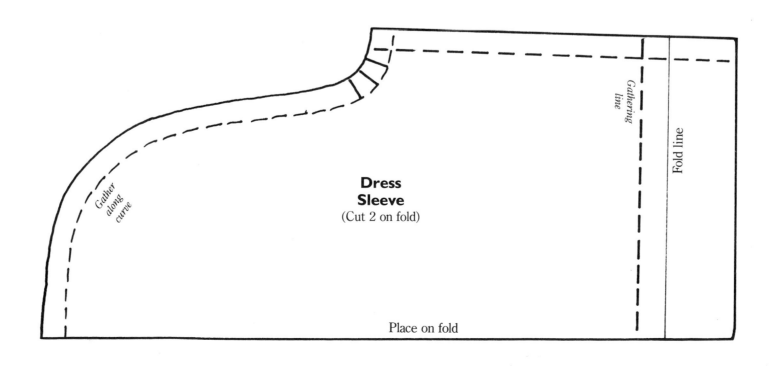

*Gather
along
curve*

**Dress
Sleeve**
(Cut 2 on fold)

*Gathering
line*

Fold line

Place on fold

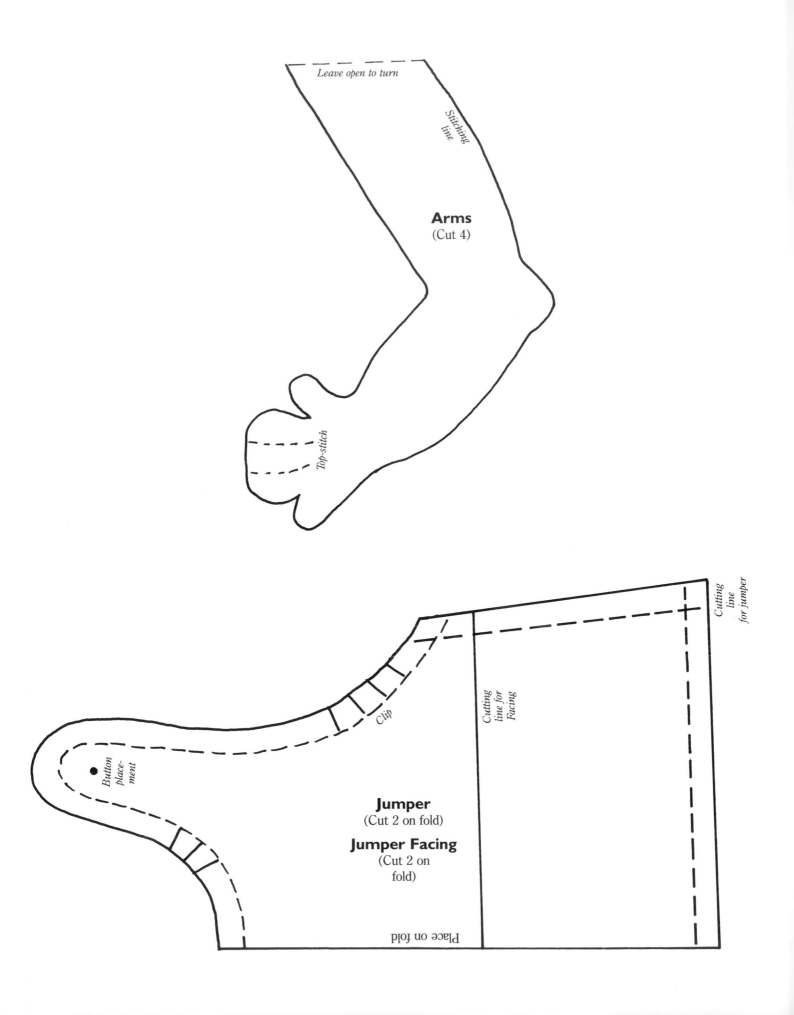

Leave open to turn

Stitching line

Arms
(Cut 4)

Top-stitch

Cutting line for jumper

Cutting line for Facing

Clip

Button place-ment

Jumper
(Cut 2 on fold)

Jumper Facing
(Cut 2 on fold)

Place on fold

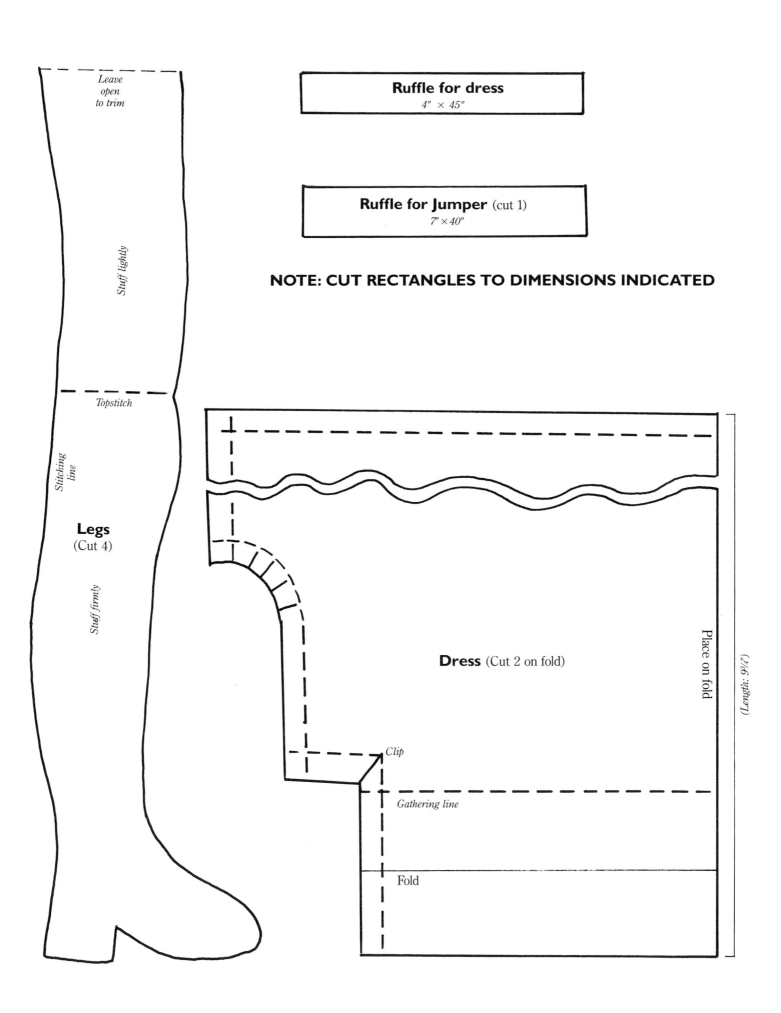

Leave
open
to trim

Ruffle for dress
4" × 45"

Ruffle for Jumper (cut 1)
7" × 40"

NOTE: CUT RECTANGLES TO DIMENSIONS INDICATED

Stuff lightly

Topstitch

*Stitching
line*

Legs
(Cut 4)

Stuff firmly

Dress (Cut 2 on fold)

Place on fold

(Length: 9¾")

Clip

Gathering line

Fold

Storybook
ANNE OF GREEN GABLES

by Christine Shively

Christine started dollmaking when she was nine. She began sewing doll clothes for her Barbie and dressed her in historical costumes rather than fashion clothes. Much of her dollmaking enjoyment comes from creating historical or folk costumes.

Christine has a degree in art from Kansas Wesleyan University in Salina, Kansas, but went back later to acquire a teaching certificate. She taught art for four years. She and her husband eventually went into business—a business spawned by her dollmaking skills. They frequently travel, which reminds Christine of her childhood vacations. She remembers packing her dolls to travel with her then and finds it amusing to be traveling with dolls still.

Christine's dolls portray many storybook characters. In discussing her creation for this book, she writes: "A special request from a friend to create Anne for her best friend set me in motion. Naturally, I had to discover who Anne was, so I curled up with Lucy Maude Montgomery's collection of stories about the adopted girl from Prince Edward Island. Her inquisitive nature, along with the qualities of honesty, thriftiness, resourcefulness, and imagination, combined with a joy of finding drama in everyday life—how could I resist her! My challenge was to make the bundle of energy created in the mind of the reader into a tangible doll. As with most of my work, the ideas began to flow as soon as fabric was in hand, and thread and scissors beckoned."

MATERIALS LIST

1/3 yard of muslin for the doll body and arms
2/3 yard of fabric for the dress
1/8 yard of black fabric for the shoes
1/2 yard of fabric for bloomers
1/4 yard of fabric for the doll's legs
2/3 yard of fabric for the pinafore
l/2″-wide lace, 1″-wide lace and 2″-wide lace for the pinafore
1-1/2″-wide lace for the dress
9″ × 14″ piece of upholstery fabric for the carpetbag
16″ of 1/2″-wide braided trim for carpetbag handles
Cream crochet thread
1 skein four-ply yarn (reddish brown)
White acrylic fabric paint
Small paintbrush
Pink powder blush
Anchor embroidery floss (#0371—medium reddish-brown,
  #09—light coral and #0262—medium olive green)
Bag of stuffing
Black and brown fine-tip permanent-ink marking pens
1/4″-wide elastic
1/4″-wide lace for the shoe tops

6″-wide straw hat
1/2″-wide ribbon to embellish the hat
3 Small ribbon roses
Green satin leaf
Small piece of corrugated cardboard
12″ of 3/8″ wooden dowel
Scrap of suede leather
Long blunt craft needle

CONSTRUCTION

Body

1. Trace the head/torso outline onto the right side of the fabric and transfer the face (see B4 or B5).

2. Embroider the face, referring to C7 and C8. Use a black fine-tip permanent-ink marking pen to draw a curved line around the iris, to darken the pupil, and under the eye. Use a very small paintbrush to apply white fabric paint around the outside of the iris. Use the brown fine-tip permanent-ink marking pen to stipple a few freckles, and apply pink powder blush.

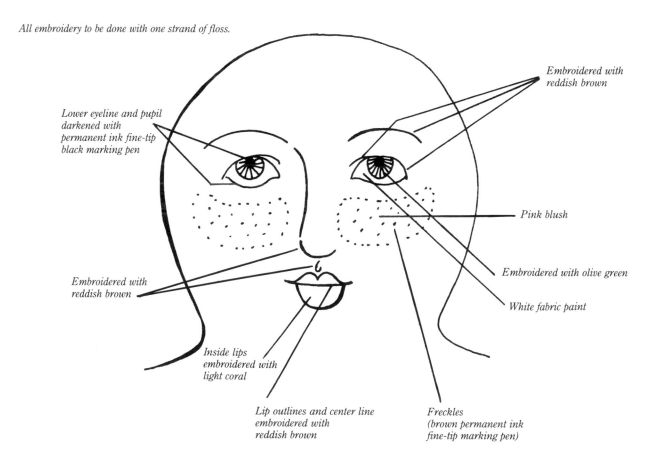

All embroidery to be done with one strand of floss.

Embroidered with reddish brown

Lower eyeline and pupil darkened with permanent ink fine-tip black marking pen

Pink blush

Embroidered with olive green

White fabric paint

Embroidered with reddish brown

Inside lips embroidered with light coral

Lip outlines and center line embroidered with reddish brown

Freckles (brown permanent ink fine-tip marking pen)

3. Attach the boot to the leg as described at E2.

4. Follow the instructions at E3 and use a 1/8″ seam allowance to stitch the torso, the arms and legs. Stuff the arms according to the instructions at E4. Stitch across the elbow from seam to seam and the knees, with the toes pointed forward (see E9). Finish stuffing the arms and legs to the top.

5. Insert the arms and the legs into the torso according to the directions at E14.

6. Split the four-ply yarn so you will be working with two-ply yarn. This gives the yarn a softer and wavier effect.

7. Draw a line on the back of the doll's head to use as a guide, and apply the yarn hair as instructed at F9.

Clothing

1. Make the pantaloons for Anne by following the instructions at G1 (Steps 1, 4B and 5A). Stitch lace to the lower edge of the pantaloons and continue with Steps 6-7.

2. Make Anne's dress by following the directions at G3 (Steps 1, 2B, 3), then follow G1 (Step 5A) and stitch lace to the edges of the sleeves. Resume G3 (Steps 5 and 8), then thread a needle with narrow ribbon to go through the sleeve casing.

3. The pinafore can be sewed by following directions at G9 (Steps 1-11 and 14-18).

Carpetbag

1. Serge along the edges of the bag or zig zag them to prevent the upholstery fabric from unraveling. Fold the raw edges of both long sides of the bag in 1/2″ toward the wrong side. Press them and turn 1/4″ of the raw edge under. Stitch on both sides to create a casing.

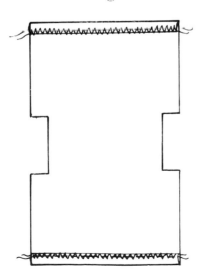

2. Cut the braid trim in half, turn under 1/4″ of each end and stitch 2″ from the sides and 1-1/2″ from the casing.

3. Fold the bag in half with the right sides together and stitch up each side 1-3/4″ from the lower notched corner.

4. With the right sides of the bag together, fold the inner corners of the bag, matching the side seam and bottom fold.

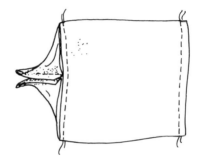

Stitch across to form a gusset. Repeat this step for both sides of the bag.

5. With the bag inside out, cut the cardboard to fit the bottom of the bag. Use the gusset seams as a guideline. Glue the cardboard to the bottom of the bag and turn the bag right side out.

6. Cut the dowel into two 6″ lengths and slide them into the casings. Turn the raw edges inward and glue them in place.

7. Lightly stuff the bag with polyester fiber.

8. Cut out the leather closure and glue it to the bag, starting at the casing seam. Fold it over the bag opening to the other side.

Hat

1. Wrap a ribbon around the crown of the hat and tie a bow in the back. Glue the ribbon in a few places to keep it from slipping off the hat.

2. Cut the satin leaf into three pieces and trim them into small leaf shapes. Glue them to the hat with the ribbon roses arranged around the bow.

3. Use the fine-tip permanent-ink marking pen to cover the white thread at the front of the shoes. Thread a needle with the crochet thread and make X's down the boot fronts. Cover the top of the boots with the 1/4″ lace and stitch or glue the lace in place.

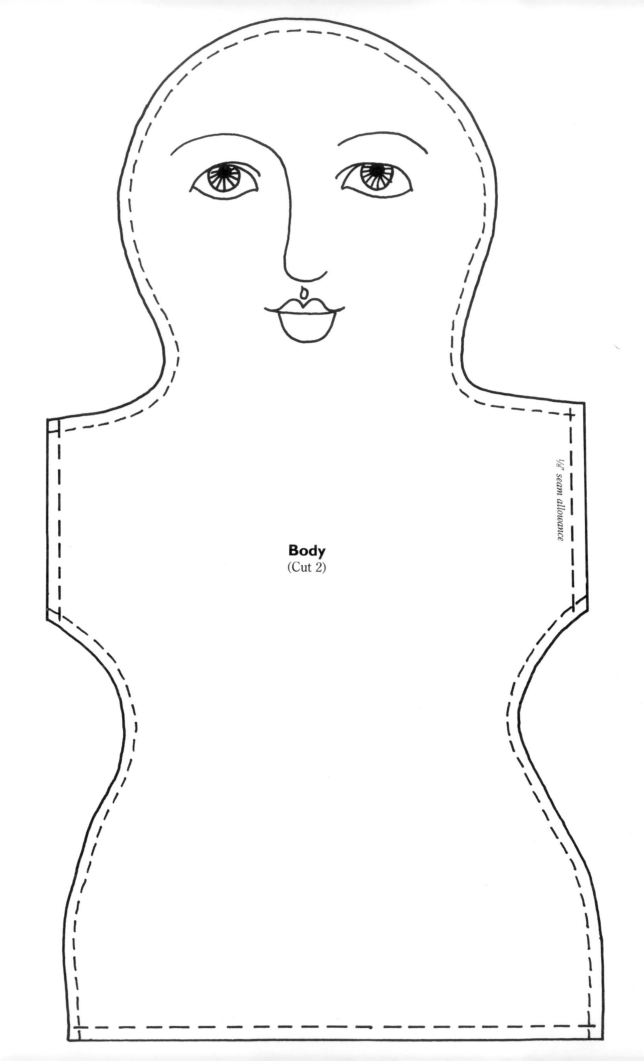

Body
(Cut 2)

⅛" seam allowance

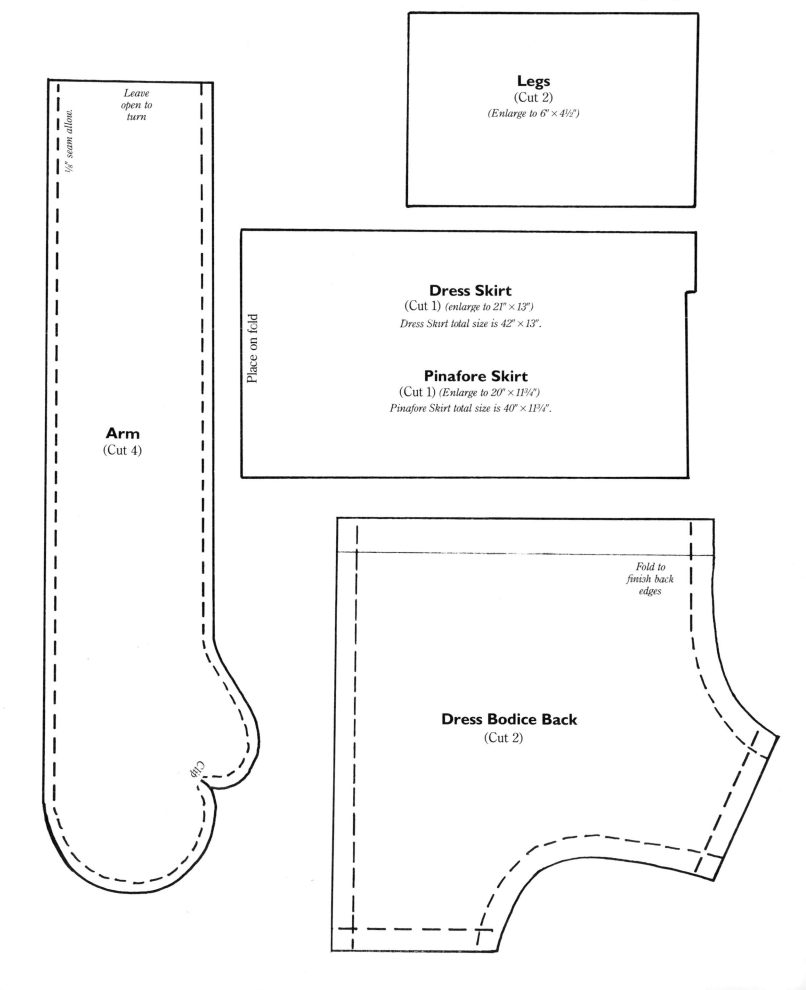

NOTE: CUT RECTANGLES TO DIMENSIONS INDICATED

Legs
(Cut 2)
(Enlarge to 6" × 4½")

Leave open to turn

⅛" seam allow.

Arm
(Cut 4)

Cut

Place on fold

Dress Skirt
(Cut 1) *(enlarge to 21" × 13")*
Dress Skirt total size is 42" × 13".

Pinafore Skirt
(Cut 1) *(Enlarge to 20" × 11¾")*
Pinafore Skirt total size is 40" × 11¾".

Fold to finish back edges

Dress Bodice Back
(Cut 2)

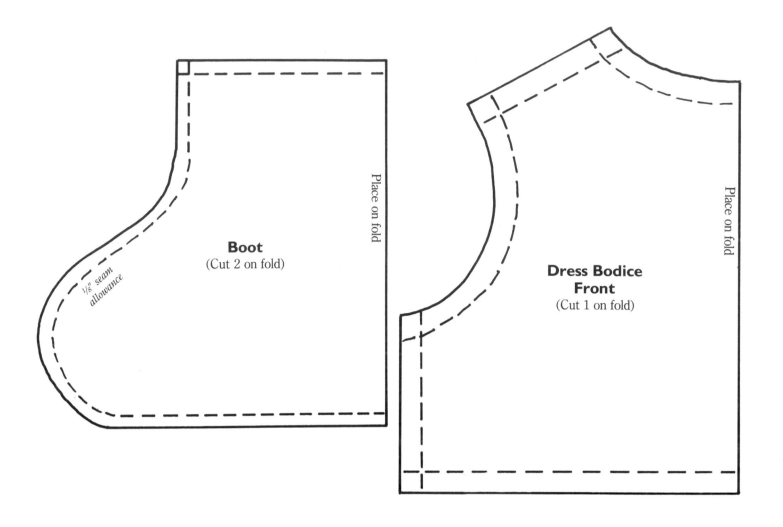

Boot
(Cut 2 on fold)

⅛" seam allowance

Place on fold

Dress Bodice Front
(Cut 1 on fold)

Place on fold

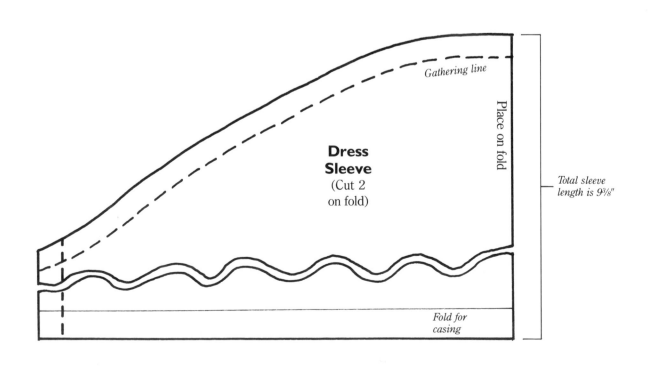

Gathering line

Dress Sleeve
(Cut 2 on fold)

Place on fold

Total sleeve length is 9⅜"

Fold for casing

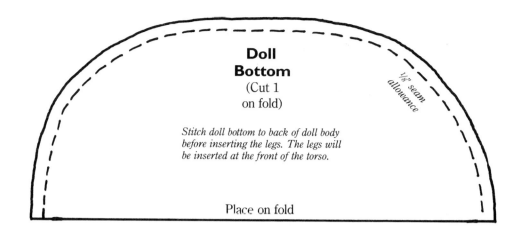

**Doll
Bottom**
(Cut 1
on fold)

1/8" seam allowance

*Stitch doll bottom to back of doll body
before inserting the legs. The legs will
be inserted at the front of the torso.*

Place on fold

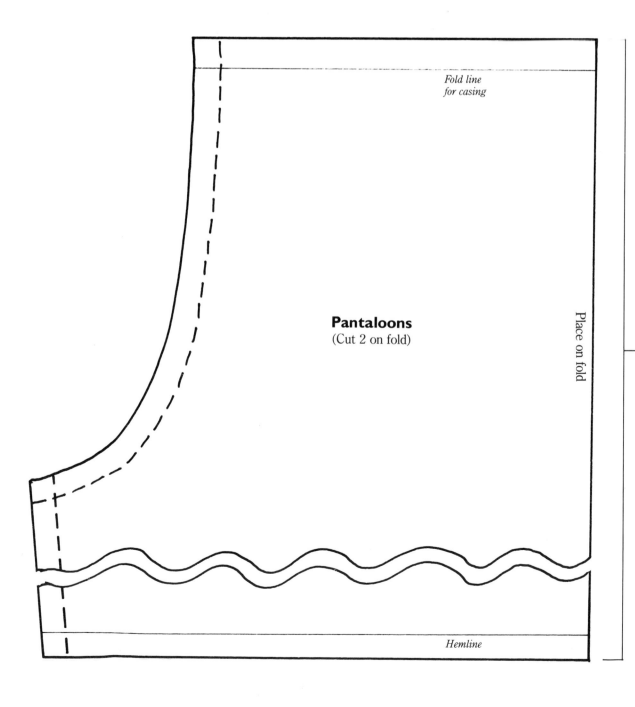

*Fold line
for casing*

Pantaloons
(Cut 2 on fold)

Place on fold

*Lengthen to
12⅞"*

Hemline

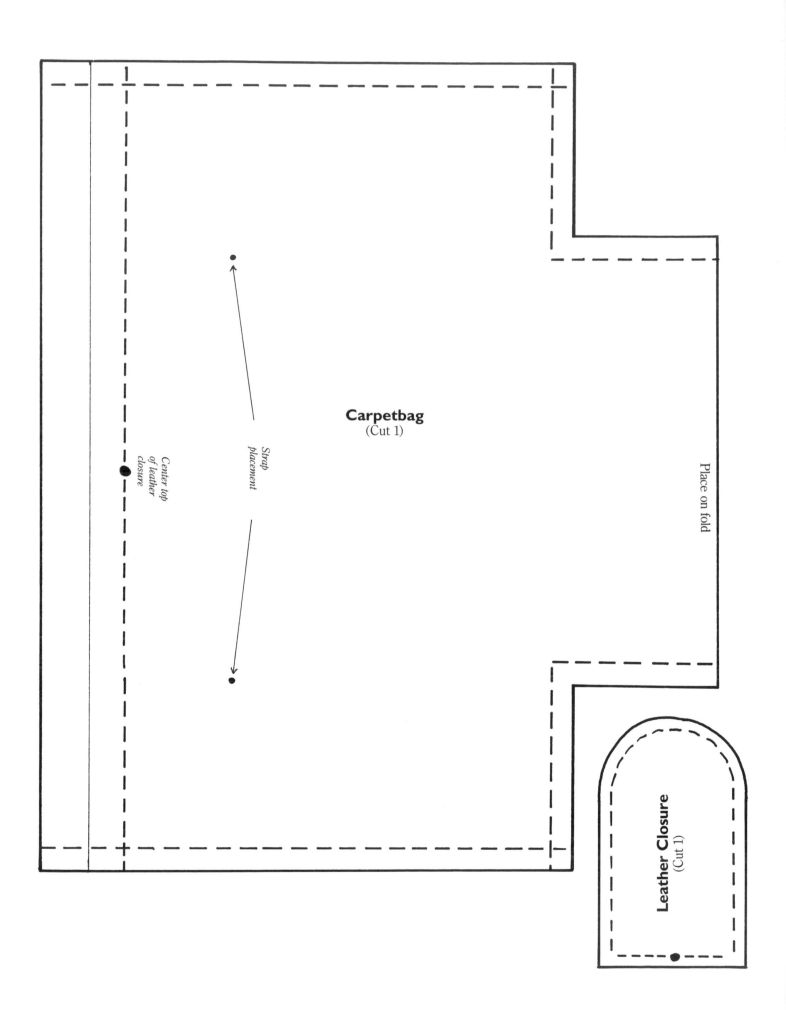

Carpetbag
(Cut 1)

Strap placement

Center top of leather closure

Place on fold

Leather Closure
(Cut 1)

NOTE: CUT RECTANGLES TO DIMENSIONS INDICATED

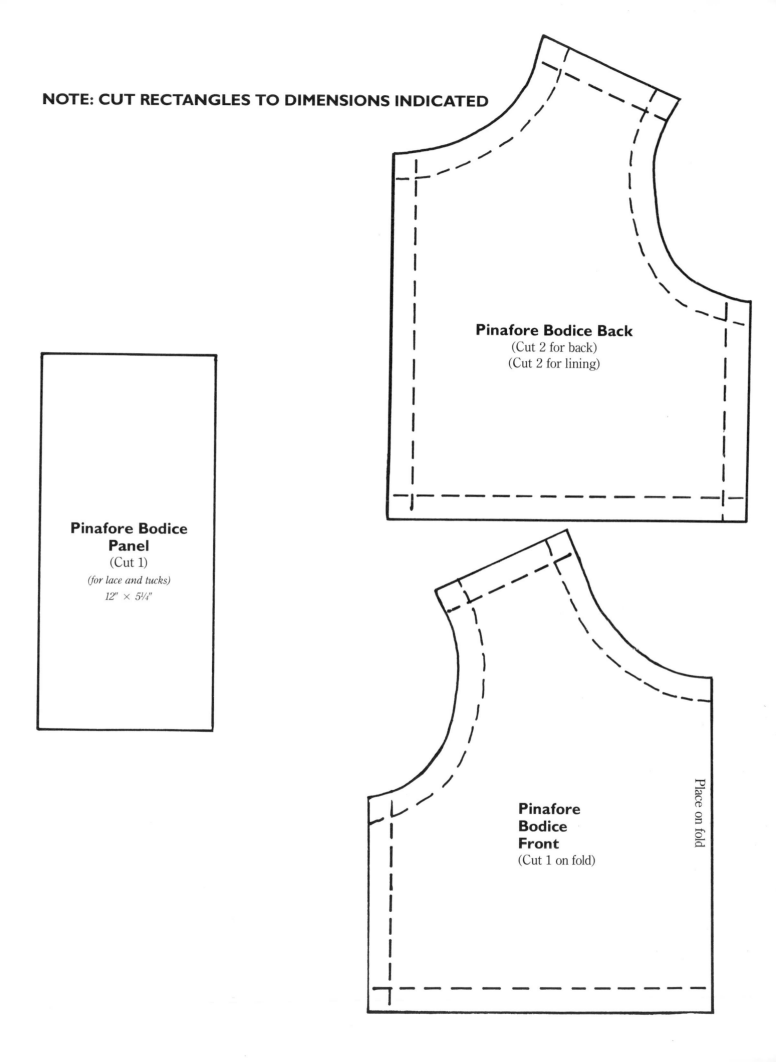

Pinafore Bodice Back
(Cut 2 for back)
(Cut 2 for lining)

**Pinafore Bodice
Panel**
(Cut 1)
(for lace and tucks)
12" × 5¼"

**Pinafore
Bodice
Front**
(Cut 1 on fold)

Place on fold

Victorian
SPRING PROMENADE

by Becky Tuttle

Becky Tuttle is one of several people who influenced me most when I first began designing. I was awed by her ability to select fabrics and combine them in such amazing and wonderful ways. Becky's style of creating soft-sculpture animals was copied by many but remains uniquely hers.

When I first asked her to create a doll for a special exhibit, she was hesitant. Becky hadn't been able to create many projects just for personal enjoyment, but she designed a whimsical Victorian doll and called her Selina Amelia de Chocotina. The doll was bending over a silver tray of chocolates with her hand outstretched, poised to nab one of the delicious morsels below her. Selina was dressed in a dark green print with black lace softly gathered around her throat. Hanging from her waist, attached to a crazy-quilt belt, were several minute tools of her trade—a small pair of scissors, a miniature sewing machine and other items. Her vibrant red hair, piled softly on top of her head, was styled in a manner typical of turn-of-the-century women. A small cat was standing on an antique doll-size needlepoint rug, watching Selina. A framed, hand-written poem proclaimed: "Selina Amelia called out to her cat, 'Oh Pussy, dear pussy, I'm growing so fat. I do enjoy quilting—no calories in that—it's just I can't resist my chocolate.'"

Becky has made several doll patterns since that day—each bearing her signature of beautiful fabric choices, well-crafted features and a look that appeals to almost everyone. She has perfected the art of looking for special trims and trinkets which make a doll unique. She selected organdy ribbon, silk ribbon and beautiful batiste lace from which to create the doll for this book. This doll gives us many clues about the kinds of things that appeal to Becky.

MATERIALS LIST

1/6 yard of flesh-colored cotton fabric for the face and arms
Scrap of striped fabric for the legs
Scrap of black fabric for the boots
2 packages of curly wool crepe hair (24″ total)
Black fine-tip permanent-ink marking pen
Embroidery floss (Anchor #968—light pink and #976—
    light blue)
Fabric paints (black and white)
1-1/2 yards of 8″-wide batiste lace for the dress and the
    pantaloons
1 yard of eyelet lace for the petticoat
Scrap of white cotton for the torso
Scrap of white lace to cover the top half of the torso
6″ of 2″-wide eyelet lace through which ribbon may be woven
1/2 yard of 2″-wide lace to embellish the back of the dress
3 yards of 1/2″-wide white organdy ribbon
8″-wide white crocheted doily
2 yards of 1/4″-wide silk ribbons (1 yard each of mauve and
    white)
1/2 yard of 1/4″-wide mauve silk ribbon
3 silk ribbon roses (mauve)
Wire parasol form
Small assortment of dried flowers
1/2″-wide enamel button
Green dried moss

CONSTRUCTION

Body

1. See B1 to trace the face and arm pattern onto the flesh-colored muslin. Trace the torso onto white fabric. Transfer the facial features onto the muslin with a #2 lead pencil, then re-trace the features with a fine-tip permanent-ink marking pen. Place a second layer of muslin underneath the face. Embroider the iris of the eye with a single strand of blue embroidery floss and the lips with a single strand of pink embroidery floss. Paint the pupil black and highlight it with a small dot of white fabric paint.

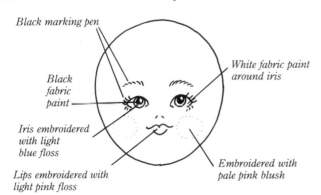

Black marking pen

Black fabric paint

White fabric paint around iris

Iris embroidered with light blue floss

Lips embroidered with light pink floss

Embroidered with pale pink blush

All embroidery to be done with one strand of floss.

2. Cut out the face, leaving a 1/4″ seam allowance, and place the face and a piece of the flesh-colored muslin with the right sides together. Stitch around the head, leaving a 1-1/2″ opening toward the top of the head for turning. Turn the head right side out and stuff it (see E4-7). Apply pink powder blush for the cheeks.

3. Attach the lace to the torso upper half and proceed at E3. Stuff the torso and the arms (see E4). Attach the arms (see E17, Step 4) and head to the torso as detailed at E11.

4. Cut the legs from striped fabric, such as ticking, to simulate stockings. Stitch them to the boots as instructed at E2.

5. Insert the legs in the body, referring to E15.

6. Attach the doll's hair following the directions at F12.

Clothing

1. Sew the pantaloons (described at G1, Steps 1-2, 4C and 6-7) and place them on the doll.

2. Cut a petticoat from 8″-wide eyelet lace which is 36″ long. Cut a skirt from organdy lace which is the same size as the petticoat. Fold the skirt in half with the right sides together and stitch the back seam of the skirt together. Stitch the petticoat in the same manner as for the skirt. Place the petticoat, with the right side up, underneath the wrong side of the skirt and stitch through both of them with a long machine stitch. Gather the skirt and petticoat to fit the doll and hand stitch them to the doll's waist.

3. Cut a 12″ piece of the 2″-wide lace for the back of the skirt. Use a needle and thread to gather it to 5-1/2″. Fold the raw ends of the lace under and stitch them by hand. Tack the lace to the sides of the doll's hips (on the skirt back) so the lace drapes down in a U.

Gather the remaining lace to 3-1/2″ and place the lace over the upper edge of the first lace. This forms a bustle.

4. Thread a piece of the wide mauve silk ribbon in and out of the 2″-wide eyelet lace and place the lace around the doll's waist, stretching it as much as you can and overlapping it in

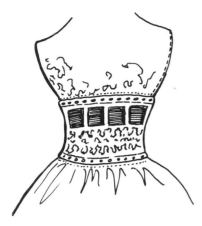

the back. Hand stitch the lace to secure it and use a needle and thread to stitch the lace at the sides, forming small darts, to enhance the doll's waistline. Tie a silk ribbon (wide) into a small bow (1-1/2″ wide) and stitch it to the back of the doll at the top of the bustle. Make a smaller bow of the 3/16″ ribbon, using both mauve and white, stitching it on top of the first bow. Stitch three silk ribbon roses below that. The ribbon roses should have a tiny bit of green silk ribbon for the leaves.

5. Fold a 1-1/2″ scrap of batiste lace in half, gather it to go around the doll's neck and stitch it in place, overlapping and folding in the raw edges at the back of the doll's neck. Place a narrow piece of silk ribbon (3/16″-wide or less) around the lower edge of the ruffle and stitch it together at the back of the neck. Stitch a beautiful button at the front of the ribbon for the doll's brooch.

6. Place the organdy lace with the right sides together and cut out the sleeves. The lower edge of the sleeves should be on the bottom edge of the lace so you will not have to hem them. With the right sides of the sleeves together, stitch around both edges of the sleeve. With a needle and thread, hand gather the sleeves from the end of the forearm upward, on both sides.

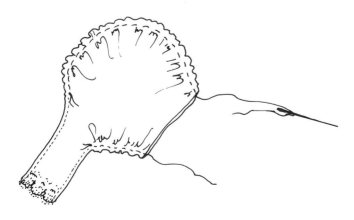

Gather the sleeve sides only slightly. Place the sleeve on the doll's arm to see how much the sleeves need to be gathered, then tie a knot in the thread. Hand gather the upper edges of the sleeve to about the circumference of a penny. Place the sleeve on the doll and turn the raw edges inside. Stitch the sleeve to the upper torso, near the shoulders.

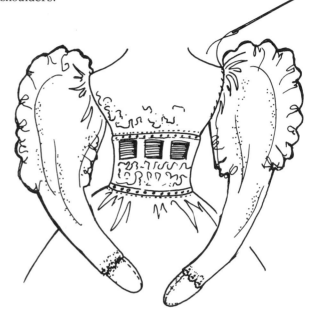

7. Thread a medium needle with the narrow white silk ribbon and make three blanket stitches at the front of each boot. Leave enough ribbon to tie a bow at the top of the boot.

Parasol

1. Wind the batiste ribbon tightly up the handle of the parasol. You may have to glue the beginning to secure the ribbon. When you get within 2″ of the top of the parasol, wind and twist the ribbon so it is looser at the top.

2. The batiste ribbon is then wound once at the center and out to the edge of the wire frame, then back to the center. This is repeated four times for each section of the parasol. When the parasol is covered in this manner, stitch the end of the ribbon toward the center of the parasol. Place the crocheted doily on top of the parasol and hand tack it to each point of the parasol.

3. Glue a nest of green dried moss at the top of the parasol. Glue dried flowers to the moss, tie two bows—one of the large ribbon and one of the narrow ribbon—and glue them to the center of the arrangement.

4. Cut four 14″ lengths of narrow ribbon (two of mauve and two of white ribbon) and tie them together in the center. Tie knots in each of the ribbons 2″-3″ apart.

Glue the large center knot at the center of the parasol where the ribbons will dangle freely.

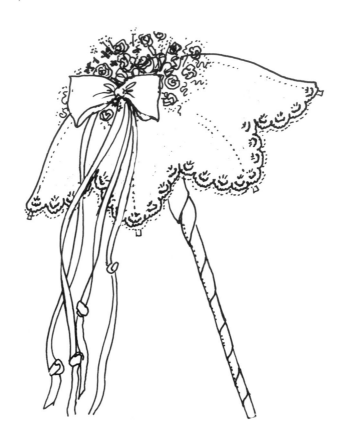

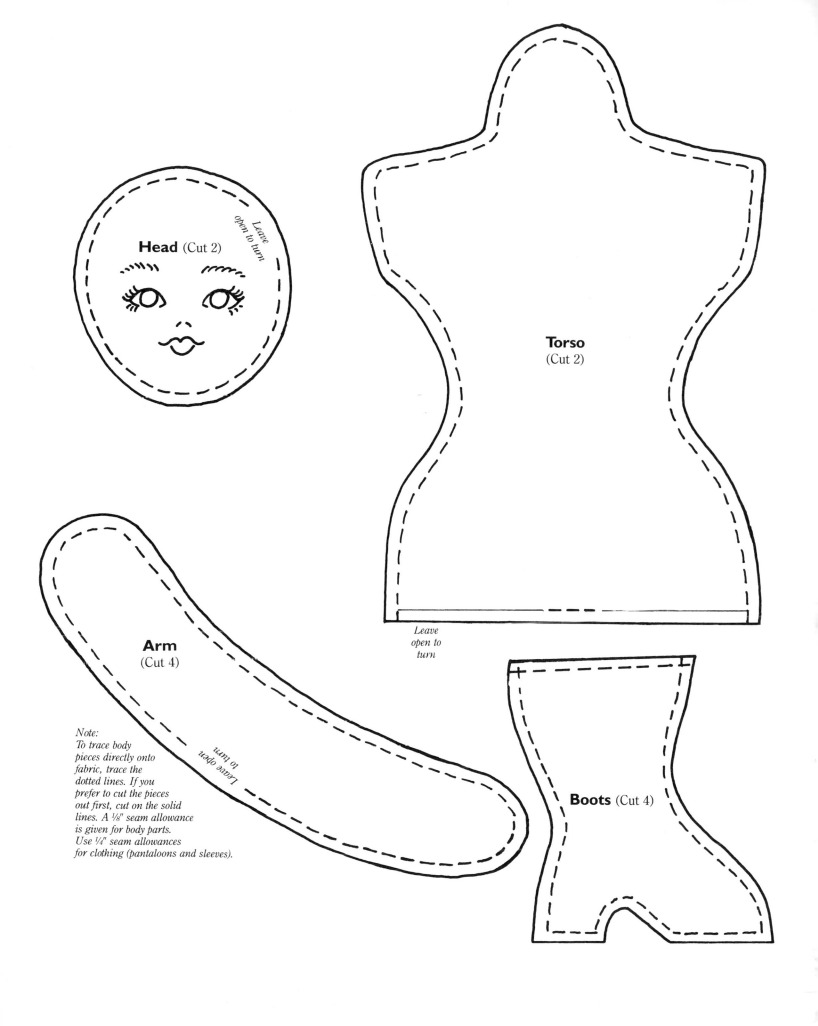

Head (Cut 2)

Leave open to turn

Torso
(Cut 2)

Leave
open to
turn

Arm
(Cut 4)

Leave open to turn

Note:
To trace body
pieces directly onto
fabric, trace the
dotted lines. If you
prefer to cut the pieces
out first, cut on the solid
lines. A ⅛″ seam allowance
is given for body parts.
Use ¼″ seam allowances
for clothing (pantaloons and sleeves).

Boots (Cut 4)

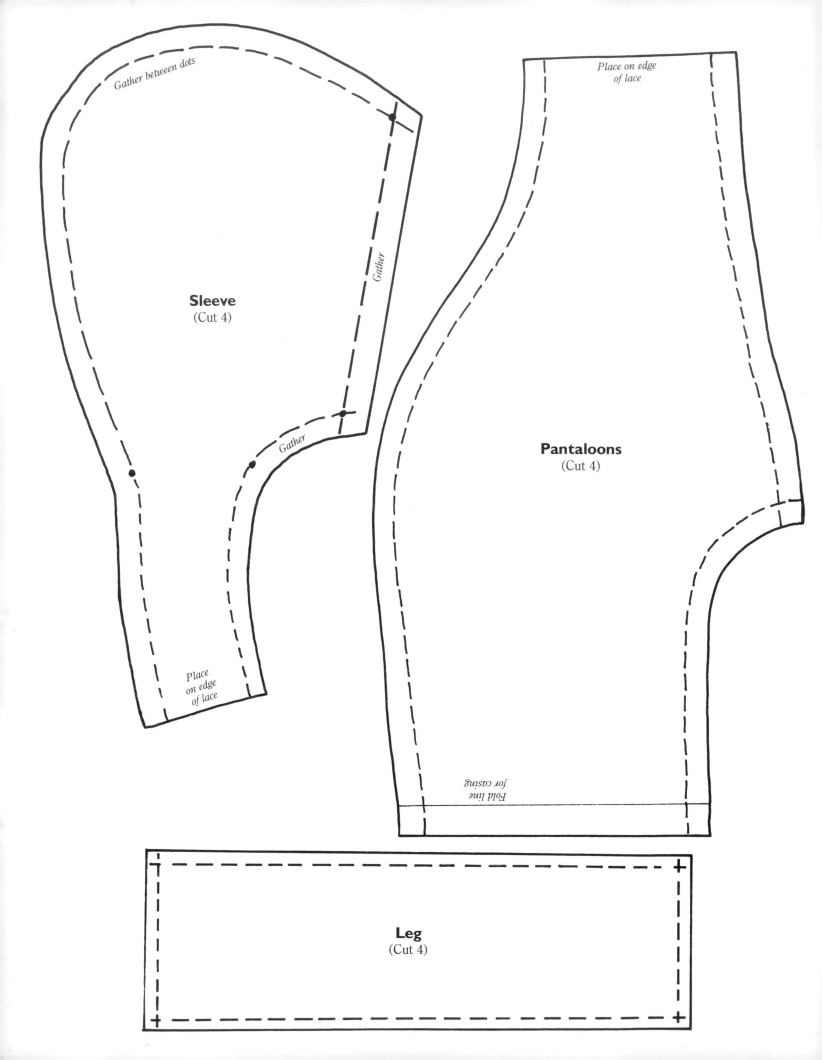

Sleeve
(Cut 4)

Gather between dots

Gather

Gather

Place
on edge
of lace

Pantaloons
(Cut 4)

Place on edge
of lace

Place on edge
of lace

Fold line
for casing

Leg
(Cut 4)

Chapter 4
ACTIVITIES

Since you have studied various dollmaking skills, you are now ready for practical classroom application. There are ample opportunities to teach others in your community, since dollmaking is of universal interest. You can start classes in your shop or home, advertise with local quilt guilds or rent space for an afternoon to hold dollmaking workshops. I have frequently taught at a doll museum which is near my home. You may even form a cloth doll club which meets in a local shop or home.

Adults are not the only people to consider when you are organizing dollmaking classes. Children are eager students and have such fertile imaginations that they may teach *you* a few new tricks. I had two important teaching experiences with children that gave me a new perspective for teaching them. The first experience occurred about three years ago, when I was designing some Christmas items for a fabric company. My son Clinton, who was six years old, asked me if he could sew something to earn some money for himself. I wasn't sure how to answer that questions, since I didn't want to squelch his creative drive, yet I knew that fabric companies might not be interested in featuring children's sewing projects in their showrooms. I finally told him I'd think about it, then decided to sew a fabric Christmas tree and let my children create the elves. I cut out several gingerbread-man shapes and stitched them together on my sewing machine. Clinton and Thomas were old enough to stuff their own dolls, but Vanessa, only three, needed my help. I stitched all the dolls and let the children paint the faces and hair. I created some pointed caps, two pair of simple trousers and one T-shaped dress. We dressed them, took pictures of them and mailed them. A few days later, I had several delighted calls from my friends at the fabric company, telling me how popular the dolls were. In fact, one of these friends said the dolls were going home to live at her house after their showroom stay was over. From this experience, the Basic Rag Doll of Chapter 1 evolved.

Last year, in a moment of guilt over not being involved in the PTA and my children's other school activities to the extent I would like to be, I decided to make a special presentation to each of my children's classes. I took ten cloth dolls from an exhibit which I co-ordinated, and my new computerized sewing machine (which my twelve-year-old son, Thomas, had taught me to program). I arranged to go to the first grade, the third grade and the sixth grade. To prepare for this, I cut squares of various colors of fabric and filled a box with beautiful rayon and metallic threads. At each classroom, I started with the machine demonstration. I purposely sat a boy at the machine first to show the children that using a sewing machine has no gender barriers. I asked each of five or six children their favorite football team or their own first names and programmed this information into the machine. I let each child press the pedal to sew the words they selected. When I told the class to return to their seats for the next part of the presentation, there were many who were disappointed because they didn't have a turn, but their interest was piqued when I opened the box and took the dolls out. I walked around the room so each person could see the doll while I told the class about each doll and its creator. All the children seemed to enjoy the presentation; a few boys followed me home to ask if they could play with my machine. "Play" was the magic word that made me realize that, if children *and* adults could view sewing as play, they would never find it tedious.

Children and adults need to derive enjoyment and stimulation from the classes they take. Adults' motor skills are more advanced, and their comprehension may be more sophisticated, but many of the teaching approaches for each group are similar:

1. Make sure your materials lists are complete and your students are given a list of the items they need to bring to class. This list may be handed to them when they register for the class. (If the class is for children, suggested age levels should be included in the publicity.)

2. You must be clear on the cost of the class and the supplies, especially if the supplies are not included in the class cost. The date and time of the class should be included in all publicity. It is wise to require prepayment of class fees.

3. Order your supplies well in advance and have a finished doll on display during the sign-up period and class time.

4. Choose a teacher who will be appropriate for the audience. Some teachers will be at home with children, and some may be more at ease with adults. Those who teach children must know how to explain procedures without talking down to them.

5. If you are teaching, outline the points you wish to make in logical sequence and be prepared to demonstrate several techniques. Make sure all the students listen to the instruction. You may want to have the children repeat the steps back to you to be sure they understand them. Ask

people to stop what they are working on so they can see you demonstrate the next step.

6. Promote family activities by having mother/daughter classes or family contests. You might, for example, offer a prize to the best family-made manger scene using the Basic Rag Doll pattern. Encourage families to involve all the children. As you can see on page 32, even my three-year-old, Michael, wanted to participate when my other children made dolls for this book. What a child makes is not as important as whether he feels included. You may also offer to teach crafts at a birthday party or train Cub Scout and Girl Scout leaders or other community youth leaders by holding an afternoon of make-it and take-it demonstrations. Whatever the age or skill level, teach your students that they don't have to color within the lines.

CLASS OUTLINES

CHILDREN'S BASIC RAG DOLL CLASSES

(Three 2 1/2-hour classes)
Suggested age: 6-12 years

Class I
Simple sewing and stuffing techniques

Have the student bring
Basic sewing kit, consisting of the following supplies:
    Small blunt-end scissors which will cut two layers of cloth
    Pincushion
    Quilting pins
    Medium-size needle
    Ecru thread
    1/4″ dowel (for stuffing)
    Tape measure
Sewing machine (This item is optional. You may want to stitch the dolls together before the class if you don't have enough space for sewing machines. If you require the students to bring a machine, ask the parents to help with set-up and to assist their children with the machine.)

Supplies to be furnished by the shop or the teacher
Muslin
Stuffing

Goal To teach the students to pin the pattern to the fabric, cut it out, stitch around the body, clip it and turn it right side out, then to stuff the doll. The students will then be taught to thread a needle and stitch the opening closed.

Class II
Painting and hair-making

Have the student bring
His/her doll
Apron
#2 lead pencil
Egg carton (to distribute and mix the paints in)
Skein of yarn for the doll's hair

Supplies to be furnished by the shop or the teacher
Fabric paints
Paper cup of water
Paper towels
Paint brushes (two or three sizes for each student)
Tacky glue
Paper

Goal To teach the students to design a face by first sketching it on the paper, then using the pencil to draw the face on the muslin. You will teach how to paint the doll's face and a shirt or blouse for the doll. Demonstrate the hair-making technique at F7 and show how to glue the bundles to the head, or let the students decide how to make their own hair by painting it or by winding it on the doll's head and gluing it (see F10).

Class III
Clothing and embellishment

Have the student bring
The doll
Basic sewing kit
Any special trinkets or embellishments

Supplies to be furnished by the shop or the teacher
(You may wish to place some of the listed items in a kit to avoid the grabbing, pushing and shoving that might result if the items were piled on the table.)

Felt
Jewels
Embellishing paints (glitter, shiny, puffy, etc.)
Tulle
Lace
Buttons
Ribbons (glitzy, plain, wired, etc.)
Tacky glue (or a glue gun, but only if it is used by an adult)

Goal To inspire the students to use their imagination. Try not to suggest embellishing methods or materials. This might also be a good opportunity to show the students how to use a needle and thread to hand-gather a tulle skirt or headdress.

ADULT'S BASIC RAG DOLL CLASSES

(Three 3 or 4-hour classes)

Class I
Simple sewing, stuffing and sculpting

Have the student bring
Basic sewing kit (see Chapter 1, page 11)
Sewing machine

Supplies to be furnished by the shop or the teacher
Muslin
Stuffing

Goal You might begin the class by showing samples of fabric which have been tinted according to the directions at A1 and A2. If all the students have basic sewing skills, you may want to concentrate on transferring the facial detail (B4 through B6) and refining stuffing skills. Review some of the basic ideas in E4 through E7 and demonstrate one of the methods at E5. E9 will also make a good demonstration.

Class II
Creating the doll's face and hair

Have the student bring
Doll
Sewing machine
Embroidery floss and needles (if embroidery is planned for the face)
Painting supplies (see Chapter 1, "Tools and Supplies") if painting is planned for the face
Glue gun and/or tacky glue

Supplies to be furnished by the shop or the teacher
Fabric paints (if they are sold by the shop)
Embroidery floss (if it is sold by the shop)
Hair fiber or yarn

Goal To have the students choose the method of applying the doll's facial details (embroidery or painting) and select the hair fiber and method of application. Demonstrations may include techniques from C1 through C6, D1 and D2, E10 and F1 through F10.

Class III
Clothing and Embellishment

Have the student bring
Doll
Sewing machine
Basic sewing kit
Special trims and accessories
Optional: decorative painting equipment

Supplies to be furnished by the shop or the teacher
Fabric for the clothing
Ribbons
Lace
Buttons
Various trims (cording, braid, etc.)

Goal   After the basic clothing items are constructed, the students should be encouraged to embellish them to reflect their own taste and background. Suggest that each student make this doll into an heirloom doll by collecting special items for embellishment. You might want to demonstrate hat-making using Marguerite and Bernadette's hat pattern (page 107). The students will also enjoy seeing various ribbon embellishment techniques (pages 42-43). You may want to show the class how to make piping and how to insert it into the seams of clothing (page 44).

HOW TO FORM A CLOTH DOLL CLUB

I was recently able to meet with several dollmakers who belong to a cloth doll club in the San Francisco Bay area. They brought several examples of their recent creations and I was amazed at their imaginative and original dolls. They related how easily the ideas came to their minds while they were meeting with other dollmakers—how one idea would fuel another—and how all the members benefited, no matter what their skill level. We discussed the formation of their club; the following guidelines will help you to form your own successful cloth doll club:

1. Select a leader. If it's your own idea, you may need to assume that role temporarily.

2. Decide on a location. It might be the local quilt or craft shop, the library or your family room.

3. Select an evening and a time.

4. Create an attractive flyer. Use some nice line drawings of dolls.

5. Distribute the flyer everywhere you can think of, to everyone who may be interested—the quilt guild, the PTA, your church group and your friends.

6. Instruct the respondents to bring samples of their work, patterns they are interested in making, photographs from magazines or other pertinent items.

7. Start the meeting with introductions, followed by a show and tell program. Discuss the club goals, such as group reinforcement, education and a doll show at the end of the year. You may also want to select a name and a symbol or club mascot. Creating a mascot doll will give the group a focus.

8. In order to maintain good communication, you may want to establish club dues. A nominal fee of $12.00 per year, for example, will help pay for a newsletter. The newsletter may include the name and address of each member, announcements and information on special lectures.

9. You may want to have door prizes each month. The club members could purchase tickets, and a drawing would be held to choose the winner. The winner would provide the prize for the next drawing. The money from the ticket sales could go toward the expenses of inviting special lecturers and workshop teachers.

10. Board members should be elected and hold separate meetings.

11. If there are other cloth doll clubs in your area, several could co-ordinate week-end retreats to share ideas.

Above all, the doll club should provide a place for real freedom in dollmaking. Do not hamper members with a lot of unnecessary club rules. Make it a relaxing and enjoyable experience.

ADDITIONAL READING

Bailey, Elinor Peace. *Mother Plays With Dolls*. McLean, Virginia: EPM Publications, Inc., 1990.

Baldwin, Ed and Stevie. *Scrap Fabric Crafts*. Tucson: HP Books, 1982.

Blackburn, Edna. "Dyeing Gold and Yellow," *Threads Magazine* (Oct./Nov. 1985), 28-29.

Bruhn, Wolfgang, and Max Tilke. *A Pictorial History of Costume*. New York: Arch Cape Press, 1988.

Bulbach, Stanley. "Why Bother with Natural Dyeing?" *Threads Magazine* (June/July 1986), 32-37.

Erlandsen, Ida-Merete, and Hetty Mori. *The Bead Book*. Translated from the Danish by Christine Hauch and from the Dutch by Danielle Adkinson. New York: Van Nostrand Reinhold Co., Ltd., 1974.

Farago, Stephanie. *The Magic and Romance of Art Dolls*. Los Angeles: Farago Publications, 1986.

Foulke, Jan. *Doll Classics*. Cumberland, Maryland: Hobby House Press, Inc., 1987.

Goodman, Deborah Lerme. "Questions," *Threads Magazine* (Oct./Nov. 1985), 8.

Hall, Carolyn Vosburg. *Stitched and Stuffed Art*. Garden City, New York: Doubleday and Co., Inc., 1974.

Kinser, Charleen. *Sewing Sculpture*. New York: M. Evans and Co., Inc., 1977.

Northrup, Wendy. "Resisting Dyes," *Threads Magazine* (Oct./Nov. 1985), 32-37.

Oroyan, Susanna. *The Dollmaker's Notebook: Working With Sculpey®*. Parliament, Oregon: Fabricat Design, 1984.

Pringle, Helen. "Miracle Messy Mixture," *The Cloth Doll*. Mt. Shasta, California (Summer 1988), 6-8.

Rustam, Phillis A. *Cloth Dolls—A Collector's Guide*. [n.p.], England, 1980.

Taylor, E. J. *Dollmaking*. New York: Workman Publishing Co., Inc., 1987.